Psychological Change
A Practical Introduction

John Mayhew

Consultant Editor: Jo Campling

MACMILLAN

© John R. Mayhew 1997

First published 1997 by
MACMILLAN PRESS LTD
Houndmills, Basingstoke, Hampshire RG21 6XS
and London
Companies and representatives
throughout the world

ISBN 0–333–65430–7 hardcover
ISBN 0–333–65431–5 paperback

A catalogue record for this book is available
from the British Library.

This book is printed on paper suitable for recycling and made
from fully managed and sustained forest sources.

10 9   8   7   6   5   4   3   2   1
06 05 04 03 02 01 00 99 98 97

Editing and origination by
Aardvark Editorial, Mendham, Suffolk

Printed in Hong Kong

For Rhona and Sara

CONTENTS

INTRODUCTION

SUMMARY

This introduction starts with a description of what is included in this book and how it is structured. The reader's attention is then drawn to the role of examples and case studies in explaining psychological principles.

Since several differing approaches to promoting psychological change are included in this book, some reasons for all of them being effective are presented.

Like any other area of knowledge, psychology is a product of history. It has also developed in a certain community of scholars who influence each other and who are influenced by the wider society to which they belong. One way of critically appraising psychology as an intellectual discipline is to look at the effects on it of history, the scholarly community and society.

The contents and structure of the book

Psychologists have explained the nature of personal change in a number of very different ways. Three have been particularly influential. They are the humanistic, the psychoanalytic and the behaviourist. Each section of the book is devoted to one of these perspectives.

1

The chapters in each section follow the same pattern. The first chapter examines the kind of counselling or therapy each perspective has created; the second chapter looks at the way in which the perspective explains change within an individual; the third presents the insights it offers into childhood experience and problems; and the fourth and final chapter describes the perspective's theoretical or empirical background. Thus the reader can appreciate how distinct forms of psychology – humanistic, psychoanalytic and behaviourist – foster change by looking at how each can be applied to one sphere of change after another.

The chapters are purposely written so that they can be read in any order. A reader who wishes to satisfy his or her curiosity about Freud's theory of personality or to compare different approaches to childhood experience can read these chapters before turning to other parts of the book.

Not only do the four chapters in each section illustrate differing applications but they also aim to develop a practical understanding of change and how it can be brought about. It is important to appreciate how this aim is fulfilled. Those who have created psychological theories have done so in the main by observing human and (in the case of behaviourists) animal behaviour. On the basis of these observations, they have made certain generalisations about human psychology. These generalisations, when related to each other, constitute a psychological theory.

In explaining humanistic psychology, psychoanalysis and behaviourism, I have worked from observation to theory in a manner similar to that of a theorist; that is, I derive theoretical principles from examples or case studies. In some instances I have used an extended case study, in others a short example, but the purpose has always been the same – to develop the reader's understanding of the kind of human experience a theorist seeks to explain. This should make it easier for the reader to see a theory's practical application.

The three perspectives presented in this book have traditionally been seen by those committed to one or other of them as in opposition to each other. Increasingly, however, any practitioner using psychological methods has tended to use a wide range and has applied them in conjunction with each other (Lambert and Bergin, 1994). My concern therefore is to make clear the contribution each can make to our understanding of change.

All perspectives produce change

Each perspective fosters change in its own way. However, there are more general processes at work when an intervention based on a psychological theory is made. We can derive some of these more general processes from an example.

A group of schoolboys were involved in producing a play for their school, and in this play one of the characters had a bad stammer. Wishing to see this role played as realistically as possible, they approached a boy who stammered and badgered him into taking the part. When the day for the first dress rehearsal arrived, the boy, having learned his lines, walked onto the stage and, to the surprise of everyone including himself, spoke fluently and without a single stammer or hesitation.

This spontaneous, psychological change can be explained in the following way. Imagine this boy stammering for the first time. He reacts to his stammering by attempting to control it. Unfortunately he finds that his attempts at control are ineffective. If he were to think logically about what is taking place, he would say to himself, 'I've tried to control the way I speak. This approach clearly isn't working. Therefore I must look for some other way of dealing with the problem.'

The reason he does not say this is that his beliefs about the need for control are so strong that he does not question them. Rather he assumes that he is failing to use the right method effectively and that he must try harder. He is making a common mistake in human problem solving, which is sometimes referred to as 'more of the same' (Watzlawick, *et al.* 1974).

Thus a pattern begins to emerge: the first time the boy starts to stammer he tries to control it; his failure to control it makes him anxious and he tries even harder; he sees that trying even harder results in further failure; he feels even more anxious but he persists. Eventually he has practised the control of stammering so much that he loses all awareness of how he is handling the problem. This lack of awareness happens with any well-established habit. For example, climbing stairs is an activity that, once learned, becomes so automatic that there is no conscious recognition of how it is being done.

When the boy took up the role of a stammerer in the school play, he experienced a reversal of the attitudes he normally had. Instead of controlling his stammer he was encouraged to create it. When he tried to do this it disappeared.

This example can be used to help us understand why each of the three psychological perspectives described in this book can produce change even though they are radically different. If we regard stammering as a problem that needs to be resolved, we can see how the solution the boy customarily chose – control – acted to maintain it. The attitudes and beliefs he had about the nature of stammering and how to deal with it formed the context in which stammering took place. This context enabled the problem to continue. When the boy got up on the stage and was required to stammer, the problem was no longer embedded in the attitudes and beliefs that formed its natural, psychological setting. Placed in a new setting that did not maintain it as the old one had, it disappeared. Because many of his beliefs and attitudes surrounding control operated automatically and unconsciously, if someone had asked him to explain why his stammer had disappeared he would have been at a loss to give an answer.

Change of setting or context can occur whenever a problem is given a new and unfamiliar explanation offered by a psychologist. At first a person may describe what is troubling him or her in common-sense terms. These terms represent the context within which the problem normally resides. If the problem is then explained in terms of a new perspective invented by psychologists and the person concerned accepts this explanation, the problem is removed or dislodged from one context, the common-sense one, to one in which it can have an entirely different meaning. The original context keeps the problem stable. When stability is removed, change is likely to follow. Let me illustrate this process using another example, that of depression.

Imagine that you are chronically depressed; that is, your feelings of sadness and apathy seriously interfere with your life and have become persistent. Suppose you want me to help you with this problem and I ask you to tell me about it. The first thing I can say about what you tell me is that, self-evidently, it does not help to resolve the problem. The second thing I can say is that what you tell me may contribute to the maintenance and stability of the problem, being a description of the context in which it occurs. This description may actually *help* the problem to continue (Wachtel, 1991).

Of course, what you tell me about your depression is only one of many possible interpretations, accounts or 'stories'. Now as a psychologist I may wish to tell a different 'story' about your symptoms, which could be drawn from psychoanalytic, behaviourist or humanistic psychology. Whether the 'story' I tell is necessarily a valid one may not be as important as whether it actually helps you to change. Laying aside for the moment the question of whether the story derived from a theory is valid, it must of course appear to be at least a feasible one for change to occur.

Taking the principle of telling a different 'story' to extremes, suppose you are a convinced psychoanalyst who is depressed and you rely on your knowledge of psychoanalysis to describe your problem. I am inclined to think that your psychoanalytic interpretation of your present predicament is unhelpful, and I may well turn to behaviourism to dislodge your symptom from its psychoanalytic context. Similarly if you are a convinced behaviourist but depressed, psychoanalytically based treatment may have most to offer. Of course, this presupposes that, for a psychoanalyst or behaviourist in mental crisis, I as a therapist can make convincing a method of change that might be rejected.

The total change of psychological context that is exemplified in the stuttering schoolboy is only one kind of change (Bateson, *et al.* 1972), though incidentally one that is often a feature of spontaneous change (Watzlawick, *et al.* 1974). Another kind is change within a psychological context; here we work with the depressed psychoanalyst helping him or her to use psychoanalytic theory more fruitfully. This kind of change will be mentioned from time to time, particularly at the end of each section of the book where, very briefly, some links between the general principles of change discussed here and a specific perspective are made.

Theories of change and the nature of psychology

I have used the example of stammering to point to some principles of change that justify presenting radically different perspectives in the same book. We can use the example of stammering to make a number of other points about the relation between the broad discipline of psychology and the specific theories examined in this book.

If we consider where the schoolboy obtained his ideas about stammering and its control, we must conclude that he picked them up from those with whom he lived – parents, friends, teachers and so on. This community taught him his 'theory' of how to deal with the problem, a 'theory' which he came to regard as having a self-evident and realistic basis. We could also say that the ideas current in his community were a product of the kind of history the community had undergone; had it had a different history, then it would have produced a different theory.

We can draw a parallel between this boy's theory and the theories that have been developed in psychology. Those engaged in doing research and creating knowledge have also been influenced by history and the communities or societies to which they belong. With regard to the former, what is accepted by psychologists at this point in time is determined by where they are located in the historical process; what they accept now will change in the future just as it has changed in the past.

Psychologists are also influenced by the communities of which they are a part, first the academic community and then the wider community of the world at large. Like the community the schoolboy grew up in, these have imparted their own measures of truth and error to the views that psychologists hold.

Psychology, which was originally a branch of philosophy, is regarded as having begun in 1879 when the first psychological laboratory was set up at the University of Leipzig. Ever since, as a developing body of knowledge, psychology has been associated mainly with universities and has relied on tightly controlled modes of research, research which, if not actually occurring in the laboratory, has aped the methods used there. Many psychologists have adopted the same methods for studying people as other scientists have used for studying animals and objects.

In contrast to the laboratory-based academic nature of much of psychology are those theories which have formed the basis of applied psychology. These have necessarily been used by psychologists working outside the university setting who have faced problems demanding more immediate solutions than is the case for their academic colleagues. Although their theories have been tainted by the goals and philosophies of academic life, they have to be much better adjusted to the realities of personal and social problems.

The theories and views incorporated in this book straddle the divide between academic and applied psychology. Their treatment aims to be systematic and intellectually sound while at the same time offering useful perspectives on everyday experience.

Turning now to the influence of the world at large on psychologists' thinking, although the major knowledge-generating force in psychology has been academic, this is not to say that the work of psychologists has been carried on wholly independently of external influence. Those who have lived out their intellectual lives in the occasionally abstruse world of the university have tended to be white, male and middle class, and as such they have imported into their discipline certain implicit assumptions. These assumptions have sometimes been racist (Robinson, 1995), sometimes sexist (Wilkinson, 1986) and often Eurocentric (Howitt and Owusu-Bempah, 1994). Some of the processes involved in racism are described in Chapter 4, and the different processes at work in men and women, some of which are related to sexism, are explained in Chapters 2 and 7. It is important to bear in mind that psychologists can be as much subject to psychological prejudice and aberrations as others. They have sometimes been slow to recognise that they themselves are affected by the processes they study (Van Leeuwen, 1985).

In order to illustrate the role of implicit assumptions imparted by society, we will look not at racism or sexism but at an example of ageism. Carp (1969) describes how certain widely held characteristics of senility, such as confusion, depression, anxiety and rigidity, have become the basis of certain tests used to determine how senile or otherwise a person is. Applying these tests, Carp compared a group of normal, older subjects with an average age of 72 years with a group of college students with an average age of 20 to see how far one group differed from another. He found that the students were significantly more 'senile' than the elderly persons. No doubt any psychologists who use these tests without taking into account the differences found by Carp have their culturally derived assumptions about the ageing process confirmed.

At the end of each section in this book, very brief comments are made on the historical and social context in which the perspectives of humanistic psychology, psychoanalysis and behaviourism have developed. This provides a basis for critically appraising the psychological views that have been presented. This basis for appraisal is further extended in the short final chapter comparing different perspectives.

Given that psychology is a product of history (some might even say an 'accident' of history) influenced by the communities to which it belongs, one might expect more uniformity in its theories. One of the reasons for the lack of uniformity is that psychological reality has a multitude of aspects, any group of which can be selected and used to form a theory. The variety and complexity of reality also makes possible many different approaches to its description and analysis. This has in turn resulted in a variety of methods that can help people change, a variety which should be welcomed.

PART I

INTRODUCTION TO HUMANISTIC PSYCHOLOGY

In the view of humanistic psychologists there is in each and every one of us a humanity that is struggling to make itself known. However, to a lesser or greater extent this humanity does not achieve a full and wholesome expression. There are two major reasons for this. First, people are selective about those aspects of their lives they will allow themselves to look at and, second, they fail to see the true meaning of their experience and misinterpret it. The society or culture in which people live plays an active role in encouraging both selection and misinterpretation. It does this, particularly in the early years of childhood, by providing the terms and conditions under which experience is to be interpreted. In other words society, especially in the form of family members, provides the socially sanctioned ideas with which to make sense of experience. This sense, at least to some extent, will not be in line with a person's humanity.

Understanding the nature of a person's present experience has been a major aim of humanistic psychologists. They take the view that if people were allowed to flourish and mature in an ideal environment, the meaning given to experience would be free from error and would represent accurately the realities of who they are and the realities of the world in which they live. Since ideal environments obviously do not exist, this does not happen. As each person grows up there are a number of influences that create psychological biases of various kinds that affect which aspects of experience will be acknowledged and how they will be interpreted.

In spite of this humanistic psychologists firmly believe that there is a motivating force at work in everyone that constantly encourages positive change. Once the circumstances are right to see clearly, the individual will choose to move in the direction of psychological maturity and become more mentally healthy. The humanity and humanitarian values inherent in each person will then come to the fore and will naturally and spontaneously guide all thought and feeling.

The two most influential proponents of the humanistic perspective have been Carl Rogers (1902–1987) and Abraham Maslow (1908–1970). Rogers pioneered a form of therapy which makes an extensive examination of experience possible. This therapy, which was originally called client-centred (Rogers, 1951) but is now referred to as person-centred therapy (Thorne, 1991), is explained in Chapter 1. It is a means by which a client can discover within his or her private world the biases which falsify experience, which rob it of authenticity and which contribute in a significant manner to the development of psychological problems.

A person's self-image significantly influences the meaning given to experience. Rogers saw the kinds of change that took place in therapy as inextricably linked with changes in how a person regarded his or her 'self'. Progress was accompanied by the dawning recognition that certain beliefs about the self were false or inaccurate. Problems associated with the self-image and how it can change are presented in Chapter 2.

There are two primary aspects to Maslow's work. Initially he carried out extensive studies of mentally healthy people, an area of work that surprisingly few psychologists have been interested in. Some of the results of Maslow's studies are described in Chapter 4, along with some of Rogers' ideas on what has come to be known as *positive* mental health.

From the results of his studies Maslow drew certain conclusions about the nature of motivation. His theory of motivation subsequently became and continues to be highly influential. It is explained in Chapter 3, with particular reference to its implications for child and adult development. Also presented in this chapter is a more recent theory (Csikszentmihayli, 1992) examining a form of motivation that is compatible with Maslow's ideas about psychological growth.

1 PERSON-CENTRED THERAPY

SUMMARY

Carl Rogers' person-centred therapy provides a means of exploring certain personal problems that are associated with incorrect or unrealistic conceptions that a person may have about his or her personality and life.

In person-centred therapy there are certain important features of the relationship the therapist develops with the client: the therapist is genuine and sincere, demonstrates an acceptance and respect for the client and seeks to reach a thorough understanding of his or her world and problems. These characteristics of the therapeutic relationship create a climate that is conducive to the exploration of personal problems and to an understanding that can lead to their resolution.

Introduction

Person-centred therapy, originally known as client-centred therapy, was developed by Carl Rogers (1951, 1966). It is a form of therapy in which the therapist plays a nondirective role and encourages the client to discuss whatever he or she wishes. The therapist takes steps to develop a safe and secure climate in which this discussion can take place so that the client feels progressively more at liberty to describe and explore whatever troubling thoughts or emotions come to mind or need attention.

An example of a psychological problem

A young man, Richard, aged 23 years, came to a therapist seeking her help with a number of personal problems. One of the matters that Richard had difficulty with arose from his attitudes to his own sexual feelings. The factors associated with these attitudes slowly emerged in the process of therapy.

Richard's parents, although they loved him and gave him every attention, had strong disciplinarian attitudes and were deeply religious. They had what might be described as a 'puritanical' attitude towards sex. As he grew up Richard quickly learned that any curiosity he had about his own sexual feelings and impulses met with either noncommittal comment or explicitly disapproving reactions. He came to believe there was something not right about anything associated with sex. He knew that this was a subject that he could not talk to his parents about. On one occasion he related to his therapist how as a boy he had inadvertently used a crude, sexual expression in the presence of his parents. He said, 'My mother went visibly faint and my father was so shocked I think he forgot to hit me.'

Because as a boy and later as a young man Richard learned never to express any interest in sexual matters in the presence of his parents, his parents regarded him as without sexual desire. Richard returned the compliment by having the same attitudes towards his parents – *he* thought *they* had no interest in sex. When he first realised that they must have had sexual intercourse in order to conceive him, he found the idea shocking, repulsive and beyond belief.

Unfortunately Richard, in his youth, was a relatively solitary individual, and this meant that he was not party to those conversations about the nature of sexuality that normally take place in adolescent peer groups. Consequently he did not explore his feelings about sexuality with others of his own age. In any case his religious ideals, which he shared with his parents, would not have allowed him to talk frankly about an area of his life that he had come to regard as morally problematic.

The end result of these experiences was that Richard came to regard sex as something sinister and unpleasant. He thought that the sexual feelings and impulses he inevitably had from time to time were bad and wrong. These feelings undermined him. He could not accept himself or be comfortable with himself when they arose. Furthermore, since he sought always to suppress everything that had anything to do with sex – impulses, feelings, thoughts, behaviour – he remained seriously ignorant of the nature of his own sexuality. He feared taking any steps that would lead to an examination of what sex personally meant for him because he suspected he would be inevitably driven to the conclusion that he was a bad person.

When Richard came for therapy he was not aware of the nature of his problems. He was so practised at suppressing or avoiding the issue that, if any of what has been described above was conscious, it was only conscious as uneasy and mostly unde-fined feelings. However, no matter how vague or distorted his feel-ings about sexuality or how deeply buried, they still continued, in Rogers' words, as 'dark and dangerous', threatening his self-esteem and undermining his self-acceptance (Rogers, 1961).

Having in mind the difficulties of the position Richard might be in, his therapist aimed to provide him with the safety and security to explore threatening and problematic features of his life and personality. For the therapist this process of exploration is based on the belief that a close examination of current exper-ience will result in fruitful discoveries.

The truth lies hidden in experience

Although Richard's past has been used to explain the nature of his problems with sexuality, it was an examination of his unease in the present that led to the kinds of insight that we have so far described. Given the right therapeutic climate Richard could discover (and did discover) the things that caused and maintained his problems in relation to himself and his sexuality. At the commencement of therapy we could say that it was all there in his experience but he had not yet unearthed it. Initially what he was aware of was only a small, unclear representation of his problem and, because of his fears, he could not avail himself of the knowledge or information that was hidden in his experience.

Richard's discoveries illustrate how, as Rogers suggested, awareness is only a part of experience. Under the right conditions conscious access can be gained to more and more of what is lodged there. The relation between awareness and experience is represented diagrammatically below in Fig.1.1.

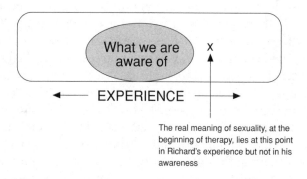

Figure 1.1 The relation between awareness and experience

There are three characteristics of the relationship that the therapist forms with the client that provide the basis for uncovering what lies concealed in experience. Using the simplest words to describe these, the therapist seeks to be sincere or genuine, to respect and accept the client and to develop a thorough understanding of what the client says and feels.

Sincerity

Sincerity is a rather simple word for what Rogers had in mind. He preferred to describe the therapist as not so much sincere as 'congruent'. Congruence is a state having three characteristics: there is freedom of access to what lies in experience; awareness is true to what experience means and is in harmony with what it means. We can use Richard's psychological state at the beginning of therapy to illustrate what is meant by this term and the demands it makes on the therapist.

At the beginning of therapy Richard felt uneasy when sexual feelings and thoughts came to mind. Any ideas he had about sex implied that he was a bad person. He could not, therefore, face up to these ideas, examine them or come to some conclusion as to what they really meant. If Richard had been brought up in more advantageous circumstances in which he could, without inhibition, have examined this part of his life, he would have developed a full and accurate understanding of the sexuality that was at work within him.

Let us suppose that Richard was well adjusted in all areas of his life except with respect to the sexual component of his personality. Let us also suppose that he became a therapist and, one day, was sitting with a client who had a problem similar to his own and who wished to discuss his, the client's, attitudes towards sexuality. We could imagine the anxieties this would generate because the client, without knowing he was doing so, might be on the brink of exploring problems that existed in Richard's personality. Richard might then become preoccupied with reducing his anxieties and coping with this psychologically threatening situation.

There are a number of ways in which Richard, as therapist, could avoid the problems the client is exposing. For example, he could direct the client away from this dangerous area. In the early stages of developing his method of therapy, Rogers learned how easily a therapist can do this. When he first began, Rogers tape-recorded his interviews and afterwards analysed what was taking place in them. He found that when his client began to explore areas of his experience where he, Rogers, had psychological problems, he would encourage the client to talk about other things. Rogers discovered that he would shy away from certain issues without being aware that this was happening.

If a client revealed to Richard (who we are presently assuming is in the role of therapist) that he felt depressed because he was having unacceptable sexual fantasies, Richard might say, 'Tell me about your depression', or, less subtly, 'Are there other things that make you feel depressed?' Here the client is asked to examine areas that are less psychologically unnerving.

Not only might Richard direct discussion away from the topic of sex but he would also have a natural tendency to use incomplete and odd ideas about the nature of sexuality as a guide to his understanding of his client. He might read his own meaning into what the client was saying and would therefore not make accurate sense of it. This would in turn set limits on how authentic his contact with his client was.

It is important that the therapist is in a position that is the opposite of Richard's. Throughout the explorations that occur in therapy, she must be as free as possible from the pressures that determine what can or cannot be said and what can and cannot be faced or understood. She must have freedom of access to her own experience and know what her experience means. Her access to her experience must not be limited or inhibited in the way in which it was in Richard. If, in Rogers' view, the therapist is congruent, her experience is present in her awareness and what is present in her awareness can be accurately communicated. Each of these three levels – experience, awareness and communication – match each other and are in harmony (Rogers, 1980).

Since Richard's therapist was, in fact, congruent, those feelings or attitudes that occurred in her as a result of her developing relationship with him were fully known in awareness. This in turn led to greater understanding of what was actually being said, and she was in tune with what was 'really' happening in each therapy session. From moment to moment she could deeply be the person she was at that time.

If Richard's exploration of his attitudes towards sex had proved unnerving to his therapist because she had similar problems, this would be an occasion on which she would sense that she was threatened. She would then need the courage to recognise what was going on inside her and inside Richard. On these occasions, if such there were, Richard's examination of his problems could prove beneficial to his therapist since it would lead her to make certain discoveries of her own.

Clearly we cannot expect a therapist to be as fully integrated as a complete state of congruence would imply. However, as a result of her training the therapist knew what she was aiming at, and such knowledge meant that she was not under the control of psychological processes she did not understand.

The client finds that a congruent or genuine therapist is, to use a word suggested by Rogers, 'transparent'. This describes the way in which the inner state of congruence expresses itself in behaviour (Lietaer, 1993). Because the therapist could freely express the conscious perceptions, attitudes, thoughts and feelings that occurred inside her when it was appropriate, Richard gained a clear perception of the authentic person the therapist was. He thought and felt that whatever she communicated was genuine, and, although he would not have used these words to describe what was happening, he regarded her as having clear access to the private world of her experience and what it really meant.

In fact the therapist expressed what was going on within her in a way that encouraged her client to experience and express his own psychological processes with the same freedom. She communicated that the exploration of experience could provide a useful and dependable guide for resolving problems.

Respect and acceptance

A second element in the therapeutic relationship is respect for and acceptance of the client. Here Rogers has used the phrase 'unconditional positive regard'. This attitude on the part of the therapist contrasts with attitudes current in relationships generally, including parent–child relationships. Customarily relationships are 'conditional'.

Richard's parents communicated to him by word and attitude that if he behaved in certain ways, if he was kind, affectionate and obedient, they accepted and approved of him and he could and should accept and approve of himself. If, however, he showed any interest in sex and asked questions about what it meant, they would not approve of him and he should not approve oᶠ himself.

By providing 'unconditional positive regard', the therapist offers a relationship which is, in many respects, the opposite of the relationship that Richard had with his parents. The therapist adopts a nonpossessive, caring attitude towards Richard, valuing him and his feelings and accepting him for what he is in the here and now, his confusion, anger, resentment, love and courage, and she does this 'unconditionally'.

This provides a safe context in which he can get to grips with his psychological problems. In this context he learns that he is with someone who accepts and respects him and continues to do so no matter what apparently morally dubious feelings lurk beneath the surface. It is as if he can reason, 'I see the therapist accepting me. This leads me to accept myself.' As a result he is able to face and deal with the threatening features of his personality that had been regarded with such fear.

Acceptance of the client, or what we might describe as the client's 'person' or humanity, can be distinguished from acceptance of things the client does. On the grounds of sincerity a therapist could not accept the behaviour of a man or woman who was acting cruelly or irresponsibly. A therapist would prefer to explore what leads to this behaviour rather than condemn it. Nevertheless since there is a conflict between the therapist's values and those of the client, the therapist may confront the client. This is done with the client's best interests in mind.

The same principle applies to any feelings that persist in the therapist. The client may be irritating, annoying, sceptical and so on. The therapist may wish to express his or her reactions since if they persist they will interfere with the progress of therapy. It is more important for the (congruent) therapist to be real and dependable than to offer a blanket acceptance of all the client's behaviour.

A thorough understanding

The final element of the therapeutic relationship involves the development of what is sometimes described as an 'empathic' understanding. The therapist works at understanding whatever statements the client makes *with the meaning each statement has in the client's world.* Richard's therapist avoided assuming that what he meant was the same as what she would have meant were she making the same statements. She checked her understanding, making comments or asking questions such as 'Correct me if I'm wrong, but you seem to be saying...', 'An important implication of what you have just said appears to be...' and 'You seem to feel this, do you?' She not only heard what he was saying but actively listened and made sure that she was getting clear in her own mind exactly what he meant. She attended not only to the content of what he was sharing with her but also to the emotions being expressed. On the basis of her developing understanding, she was able to communicate her accurate sensing of what he was experiencing.

As an experienced therapist who was beginning to know her client well, she was able to articulate implications of what he was saying of which he was only partially aware or sometimes totally unaware. She could comment, for example, 'When you say this, you seem to feel this', and he would reply, genuinely, after some thought, 'You're right, I do feel this – though up to this moment in time, I'd never realised it.' Besides the explicit meaning of what is being said, the therapist is able to pick up what is implicit, particularly at an emotional level. This results, for both herself and the client, in a stepping beyond the client's words and the identification of areas of his experience that he has not so far recognised or acknowledged.

The process by which the client gains from the empathic therapist can be contrasted with the processes at work when a therapist is giving advice. When I am given advice, I look at the advice, examine it and evaluate its possibilities. I do not examine my experience or avail myself of the potential that exists there for discovering what is useful.

However, when a person works at empathically understanding me and asks, 'I may not have got this quite right, but you seem, John, to be saying this and this and appear to be feeling...', then I look at my experience to see how correct this person's reflections and suggestions are. It is in the process of examining my experience that I look at it afresh, can discover things I had not noticed before and am open to learning from it. The therapist who is working at empathically understanding me is closely attending to my experience and is getting me to do the same.

There are certain dangers for the therapist in seeking to develop a profound understanding of the client's world. Richard's therapist had to remind herself from time to time that she and the client were different. If she did not have a sufficiently clear identity and awareness of her separateness from the client, there would be a danger of being seriously depressed during periods when her client was in despair or of being overwhelmed by his anxieties. On one frightening occasion Rogers (1961) had to desist from offering therapy to a client because he had overidentified with the client and was entering the client's world to such a degree that he was beginning to lose a sense of the boundaries of his own personality.

The therapist's use of his or her own reactions

Occasionally the therapist will go beyond clarifying in his or her own mind what statements the client has made or pointing out feelings of which the client is unaware and will share thoughts that arise as reactions to what the client has said. Rogers (1970) found that this often produced a surprisingly profound response from the client, who, he found, often went on to develop some significant insights.

This is in fact what happened between Richard and his therapist. Quite early on in therapy she said that what struck her when she listened to him talking was that maybe for him sex and love could not co-exist or be associated with each other. She did this even though Richard had talked about these matters only in the vaguest terms. When he thought deeply about what she had been suggesting, he realised that he could not express sexual feelings towards someone he loved since this would involve that person in something he regarded as bad. This realisation opened the door to significant progress.

In order to act in the client's best interests, there are certain principles that should guide a therapist when sharing what is going on inside him or her. This sharing must be done with the aim of promoting the client's psychological growth (Yallom, 1980). It must be appropriate in content and timing (Rogers, 1970) and not serve the interests of the therapist, who, on some occasions, may be tempted to sound off about something or impose on the client some cherished ideas. Also what is said must be owned by the therapist as a statement from his or her own perspective; thus phrases of the following type will be used – 'It seems to me...', 'I think that...' and 'What strikes me is...' – rather than phrases like 'This is the way it is...' and 'You are...'. Finally, whatever of the therapist's thoughts and feelings are introduced, they must soon be followed by a return to focusing on the client's own experience.

As Gendlin (1967) has shown, the therapist's saying what strikes him or her is a useful device for helping a client who says very little or is silent. During a period early in therapy when Richard was depressed and withdrawn, his therapist shared with him what she guessed were his feelings. She did this as empathically as possible. After a little time he began to talk more freely and became progressively more responsive.

Relations between congruence, acceptance and empathy

A person who is congruent is one who accepts his or her own thoughts and feelings. This in turn leads to a more ready acceptance of the thoughts and feelings of others. Thus there is a clear relation between congruence and acceptance.

The openness to another's thoughts and feelings implied by acceptance is a necessary ingredient for developing a deep understanding of him or her. Thus there is again a relationship between acceptance and empathic understanding.

There is also a relationship between congruence and empathic understanding. An increasingly congruent person is one who is more and more open to the flow of experience and the meaning of what is sometimes hidden within it. Therefore his or her store of self-knowledge is continually expanding. Such self-knowledge invariably helps in developing an empathic understanding of the flow of experience in another person.

Attitudes that are not helpful to the client

By looking at the therapeutic relationship as Rogers defined it, we can identify those of the therapist's attitudes and reactions that are unhelpful. We can exemplify these by looking at failures in congruence, acceptance and understanding.

One outcome of the failure to be congruent has already been explained; the therapist may find the client exploring issues that expose his or her own psychological problems, and this may adversely affect the course of therapy. Another outcome of the failure to be congruent occurs when the therapist adopts a professional façade.

When a person uses a façade, a pretence is substituted for more genuine behaviour – the person is acting in one way while inside something very different is happening. In the sphere of therapy, for example, a professional therapist may assume the façade of expert knowledge and imply that he or she knows a great deal more about the client's psychological functioning than is in fact the case. In the view of humanistic psychologists the therapist will be hiding a profound ignorance about clients and their circumstances because only they can know their own worlds. This unreal situation created by the use of a façade has a stultifying effect on the progress of therapy. Clients become involved in the unreal and unhelpful dynamics of interacting with an artificial person. For therapy to move forward the realism of the therapist must make the realism required for progress possible.

The therapist may show a lack of respect for the client in a number of ways. For example, Richard's therapist could have diagnosed him, slotting him into a single category. She could have treated him as 'typical' of any particular group of people, an ignorant student, an anxious neurotic, an uncooperative psychopath and so on. Assigning a person to any of these categories implies that everything unique about him or her is irrelevant. Ignoring all that is unique in an individual's personality is to treat that individual inhumanely and will prevent beneficial change.

Very often what accompanies the process of diagnosis or categorisation is an evaluative assessment or judgement not of the client's behaviour but of the client's personality. This process smacks of the same evaluative stance that Richard's parents took towards him, particularly with regard to his curiosity about sex. In contrast Richard's therapist took up a stance that was free from moral or diagnostic evaluation of him as a person.

Another way in which disrespect for the client may be expressed is for the therapist to interpret what the client says by stating what it really means. Doing this not only implies greater knowledge on the part of the therapist but may also be particularly problematic because, no matter to what degree it is accurate, this may lead the client to rely on the therapist's words, which will in turn prevent the more useful process of self-exploration and self-discovery. Of course, when the therapist interprets what the client says, he or she will not be involved in the process of developing an empathic understanding.

There is one other feature of the therapist's outlook and behaviour that can prove unhelpful to the client. Without any deep-rooted commitment to the client's welfare, the therapist may go through the motions of being person-centred. For example, some therapists have developed the habit of merely reflecting back to the client whatever the client says, responding with phrases such as, 'You've just said this...' and 'In other words you believe...'. This process of reflection has not been done with any genuine or authentic involvement with the client or his or her problems. Needless to say, when Rogers discovered that some therapists were doing this in the name of person-centred therapy, he was horrified.

A barrier to initial progress

The client may have certain expectations that differ significantly from those of the therapist. The client may take the view that the therapist is an expert who, with a minimum of information, can provide the correct, problem-solving advice. In contrast to these expectations the therapist seeks to provide a climate in which the client can find his or her own way. While these differences between therapist and client continue, progress in person-centred therapy is not possible. However, it is customary for the client to realise relatively quickly that the therapist will be a companion, a fellow traveller in the search for a more realistic approach to his or her problems.

Why the client makes the right discoveries and choices

If we followed closely the therapeutic process through which Richard passed, we would find him making discoveries that showed him the degree to which his limited view of sexuality was unrealistic. This view had been taught him by his parents and imposed on him, and was not one he had worked out for himself. Not only this, but we would also find that the things that he discovered for himself led him to an entirely new perspective, one that represented the true or intrinsic meaning of sexuality for him. In the process of uncovering this meaning, he found that the sexual feelings and impulses that threatened him were not a dark and dangerous spectre. He discovered the legitimacy of his own sexuality and that it was not the morally questionable thing he had always believed, nor was he the bad person he feared he might be. Thus he learned how his sexuality could play a natural and spontaneous role in the expression of his affection for the partner he had come to love.

Richard's discoveries and choices during therapy were determined not only by the context provided by the therapist but also by the inner drive within Richard himself, a drive towards greater realism and better-adjusted psychological health. Customarily clients, like Richard, discover in the process of therapy that what they suspected was bad about them turns out to be neutral or good. Even, however, where discoveries are made that involve regrettable features of the client's character or behaviour, they are accepted in a way that makes it possible to work on them and achieve change. This happens because of the inner drive for psychological health.

Humanistic psychologists such as Rogers (1978) and Maslow (1970) believed that this drive could easily be thwarted and, when blocked, would produce mental and emotional difficulties and problems. However, when a context such as that of the Rogerian therapeutic relationship is provided, in which the drive can be fully active, it always takes a person in the direction of the best possible psychological and ethical choices.

The broad implications of the therapeutic relationship

In the area of sexuality Richard's parents could have offered a more 'therapeutic' climate. No doubt in many other areas while he was growing up they *had* provided this. In these areas they would have conformed to the principles that Rogers recognised as being essential for a person-centred relationship.

The principles Rogers described can be reproduced in relationships in a wide range of spheres. Let us look at two examples, work and education. In the setting of work, if the principles of person-centred therapy are operating, people will be getting on with each other on the grounds of sincerity, respect and acceptance and a desire for empathic understanding. These grounds will give people freedom of access to what is contained in their experience, and they will be able to learn from it. Clearly this will have constructive consequences. If, for example, a person is given the opportunity to be actively listened to and empathically understood by a working colleague, this person will, by looking at his or her experience of work, discover things that were previously outside awareness. In turn the discovery of what is lying dormant in experience will lead to a more understanding and mature approach to work.

Rogers had a particular interest in teaching, learning and student–teacher relationships. Many of his ideas and the research that supports them is presented in his book, *Freedom to Learn* (Rogers, 1983). If the learning that takes place in person-centred therapy is used as a model for the learning that should take place in educational settings, the experience of the pupil or student is of more importance than the knowledge that is so often imposed. Efficient learning occurs when the student plays an active part because he or she is working in a secure atmosphere that promotes inherently human activities such as spontaneous curiosity and the desire to learn. The development of valued insights will become a natural outcome of this process. The teacher who aims to generate this atmosphere recognises that his or her major role is to facilitate and to resource learning by creating choices and options for the student. The teacher also shows his or her respect for the student by encouraging such things as participation in all aspects of the learning process and communicating the expectation that the student will make responsible choices.

2 PERSONALITY AND THE SELF-CONCEPT

SUMMARY

This chapter offers an explanation of the nature and significance of a person's self-image. Rogers regarded the self-image as an important point of reference in the personality, and for this reason a person seeks to maintain its stability and consistency.

In every relationship one person communicates to another how he or she is experienced. If a child (or adult) takes a cue from this, a self-image may be built on the basis of how a person is regarded and not according to the actual or true characteristics possessed. The origins and implications of this discrepancy are explored.

Introduction

Carl Rogers (1951, 1959) saw the progress taking place in person-centred therapy (the form of therapy he pioneered) as linked to changes in the client's feelings and thoughts about him or herself. Rogers developed his description of these changes into a systematic explanation and theoretical justification of what was taking place in therapy.

In addition to covering Rogers' views on the self, we will also look at some processes that Laing (1969) has described. These

concern the contribution that other people make to the formation and maintenance of an individual's identity.

Assessing another's personality and assessing our own

The impression we form of our 'self' is similar in many ways to
the impression we form of another individual's personality.
Another's personality is virtually always experienced as an integrated whole. In other words we do not think of another person
as made up of a number of characteristics or traits – a bit of
generosity, obstinacy, kindness and so on. Rather we have what
might be described as an overall or holistic impression.

This overall impression has several characteristics. It is made
up of attitudes and feelings that are difficult to put into words –
usually we find it difficult to describe exactly what a person is
like. Second, the feelings we have about another person are
primarily evaluative in nature; although not always consciously
recognised, these feelings often indicate the degree to which that
person does or does not conform to our fundamental values.
Third, even though it is difficult to describe an individual's
personality in words, our impression provides a significant
guide to how we should approach or deal with him or her.

We can draw a close parallel between the nature of the
impression formed of another's personality and the nature of
the impression we have of our own personalities – your view of
your 'self' and my view of my 'self'. Our view of ourselves is a
composite whole that is difficult to put into words and tends to
be evaluative in nature. It indicates the degree to which we
think and behave in ways that are consistent with our fundamental values, and it is also used by us as a guide when we
relate to others.

The self-image or self-concept

The composite impression we have of ourselves constitutes our
self-image or self-concept. Rogers regarded the self-concept as a

significant source of reference in the personality. It provides a continuous guide, informing us that the thoughts and feelings we are having or the ways we are behaving fit in with the kind of person we take ourselves to be.

Because of its role as a guide and source of reference, the self-image must remain stable and consistent, so much so that anything that leads a person to question the validity of his or her self-image is experienced as very threatening. If we are treated in a way that indicates that we are not the kind of person we assume ourselves to be, we usually feel deeply disturbed.

Not only is the self-concept a significant source of reference but it also incorporates an image of the 'self-in-relation-to-others'. This usually predicts, particularly in social relationships, how a person will behave. Therefore, change in the self-concept, when it occurs (through the process of therapy perhaps), is likely to result in change in the way a person relates to others. This will in turn affect how others relate to him or her.

The origins of the self-image

The self-image originates, in a child, through interaction with the parents. In this interaction the parents communicate how they experience the child. This in turn influences how a child experiences him or herself. For example, when a father takes the lead with his son or daughter and is dominant in their relationship, it is as if the child reasons, 'I see my father is dominant and treats me like a submissive person. He experiences me as submissive. Therefore I am.' Thus the feelings others have towards the child provide directives to how self should be regarded.

Parents also communicate how they experience particular aspects of the child's behaviour. For example, parents and other adults frequently take the view that a child's aggressive behaviour, particularly if it is directed towards themselves, is wrong and bad. A child, taking a cue from this, develops the same convictions as the parents. Again, it is as if the child reasons, 'My parents experience my aggressive behaviour as bad. Therefore it is bad.'

The parents' experience of pieces of the child's behaviour feeds into their experience of the child 'as a whole'. Since what he or she does is often regarded as the product of a particular personality, how the parents feel about what the child does indicates what kind of person they take the child to be. This in turn affects how the child feels about him or herself. For example, any aggressive behaviour suggests to the parents that the child's personality can be described as an aggressive one. Again, taking a cue from this, the child may also regard aggressive feelings and behaviour as belonging to his or her personality. This results in aggression being regarded not only as bad and wrong but also as a reprehensible aspect of the personality.

How a person communicates how another is experienced

We have established that the origins of the self-image lie in the way in which the parents communicate their experience of the child. In all relationships, including the parent–child relationship, individuals communicate their experience of each other's personalities and behaviour through acts of what are called 'confirmation' and 'disconfirmation' (Laing, 1969). The following example will be used to explain what these terms mean.

A psychologist is giving a lecture on marital disharmony and in passing makes what he feels is a rather witty, disparaging remark about certain sociologists' views of marriage. If his audience bursts into spontaneous laughter, they communicate that the meaning his behaviour has for him, let us say as an act of innocent humour, it has also for them. They therefore confirm his behaviour.

However, suppose that his audience fails to respond to his joke and one of their number breaks the awkward silence by pointedly asking why he is always poking fun at people. In this case the psychologist's understanding of his own behaviour is not the same as that of his audience: they have disconfirmed it.

Acts of confirmation and disconfirmation must be distinguished from agreement and disagreement. If, for example, you
understand an explanation of marital disharmony that I give
and then go on to disagree with it or reject it, you have nevertheless largely engaged in an act of confirmation. This is because the
meaning that my (explanatory) behaviour has for me is also the
meaning it has for you. If, however, in the course of simply
explaining something to you, you stopped me and suggested I
was making things very complicated because I wanted to show
how stupid you were, you would then be disconfirming my
behaviour – assuming, of course, that it was not my intention to
make you look stupid and therefore that my behaviour did not
have the same meaning for me as it did for you.

Acts of confirmation and disconfirmation are processes
involved in the creation and maintenance of a person's self-
concept since a person is generally sensitive to and takes into
account how he or she appears in the eyes of others. It might
be said, for example, that the spontaneous laughter of the audience confirms the psychologist's self-concept insofar as he
regards himself as having a very good sense of humour or as
being a natural wit. If they do not laugh but question his
behaviour, they disconfirm this aspect of his identity – especially so if instead of asking why he pokes fun at people,
someone asks him why he is such an inveterate sceptic.

The concepts of confirmation and disconfirmation point to a
very important form of feedback that one person gives to
another. A person's confirming influence, although extremely
important, often goes unrecognised. A person's disconfirming
influence, however, is usually felt by another to be upsetting
and disturbing. Disconfirming the psychologist's behaviour, as
we have seen, fails to maintain his self-image and can create
emotional turmoil by implying that he is not the person he
takes himself to be. Consider a further illustrative example.

An elderly and intelligent woman finds it difficult to live on
her pension. Although she has always been an honest and
respectable woman – and treated (or 'confirmed') as such by all

her friends and acquaintances – she realises one day, while in a shop looking at some tinned beans on display, how easy it would be to take a tin and leave without paying for it.

The more she thinks and imagines quietly and secretly picking up a tin, the easier such an action seems to be. In a short time and with mounting desire, actually taking a tin appears almost sensible. These attitudes and feelings, related as they are to fulfilling her needs, tend to make her oblivious of any ethical questions her projected behaviour would normally raise. Any unease over the dishonesty of her actions is clouded by her desire to obtain what can easily be taken and remains sufficiently vague for her not to consider it. And so she attempts to leave with a tin of beans.

Suddenly she is confronted with the acute shock of being caught and finds herself confused and perplexed. What disturbs her is not any sense of regret at what she has done or the threat of a future penalty. What disturbs and horrifies her is that an irate shopkeeper and a policewoman treat her as if she is a thief. This is an entirely new experience for her. She has never before known herself as a thief, not even during her recent attempt at stealing.

She is faced now with a severe threat to her self-concept, a threat too clearly expressed in the treatment she is receiving from the shopkeeper and policewoman. This treatment is not necessarily curt or verbally punitive but it does communicate to her that she is now known by others as a thief. In view of her previous experience of herself and the way others have confirmed this experience, she may at first doubt whether she is a thief and be tempted to react with indignation over the way she is being treated, but such indignation soon turns to despair as she realises she has been stealing and begins to understand her behaviour with the new meaning given to it by her accusers. To their condemnation must now be added her own as she also realises that the contempt she felt in the past for thieves she must now apply to herself.

Disconfirmation, confirmation and change

This example of an elderly woman starkly illustrates the influence of disconfirmation, an influence that in this case cannot be ignored or rejected. Even, however, where a person can, with legitimate justification, reject a disconfirming influence, this may prove to be much more difficult than at first appears. If I know myself to be an intelligent person and you treat me as a stupid one, I must at the very least draw the conclusion that I come over to some people (such as you) as stupid. Not only could this be upsetting, but actually worrying about how stupid you seem to find me may so distract me that I do in fact make silly mistakes and, as a result, justify the view you take of me.

Since confirmation of the self-image is virtually always preferred and disconfirmation where possible always avoided, it is easy to see how choice of friends and marriage partners may be guided by the degree to which they confirm the identity a person possesses. Insofar as intelligence is regarded by you as one of your valued characteristics, you will not regard someone who disconfirms it as one of your friends. You will gravitate towards those who confirm it. Friends may in this regard fulfil a more fundamental function than is normally recognised. They can maintain the stability of your self-image by constantly communicating that you are the person you think you are. Furthermore, by continuing to provide acts of confirmation a friend makes a person feel that he or she can express self freely in ways that are in line with a well-established self-image.

Unfortunately this type of friend may not always be available. If you wish to regard yourself as a highly intelligent person when in fact you are a stupid one, you might find it difficult to find people who will regard you in the way you wish. If you are continually confronted with acts of disconfirmation, you may no longer regard your high intelligence as credible and change will take place in your self-concept. Alternatively recognising that sharing what you regard as your brightest ideas is not meeting with the desired effect, you may simply become highly selective in your choice of friends or end up maintaining your self-concept but having no friends at all. Unfortunately there are a number of people who become very lonely for this reason.

We saw in the case of the elderly woman how acts of disconfirmation can bring about change. In some circumstances confirmation can also produce change. Insofar as it involves responsiveness to certain elements of a person's identity and, by implication, a lack of responsiveness to other elements, confirmation can develop or even exaggerate certain personality characteristics.

Parents very often use the processes of confirmation and disconfirmation in an effort to foster or encourage what they regard as good behaviour and to inhibit or change bad behaviour. Thus parents may tell an aggressive child, 'You are a good child and a good child is not an aggressive child. Your aggressive behaviour is not therefore in line with what we expect of you and', by implication, 'it is not what you should expect of yourself.'

Gaining the wrong impression from what you experience

If what we think of ourselves is caused by how our parents and how people such as our friends accept or reject us and confirm or disconfirm our behaviour, is there any way in which we can transcend the influence of others and become genuinely ourselves? Can we avoid, for example, the meaning imposed by our parents on our experience and find an authentic meaning that is an essential part of experience and can be found within it? Humanistic psychologists such as Rogers and Maslow believed that this is possible. In fact they regarded authentic meaning as present in the earliest stages of a person's life.

Rogers believed that when, after birth, an infant encounters the world, his or her reactions are distinctly individual and personal and experienced with a certain psychological clarity.

Responses to a new food, for example whether the food is accepted and taken in or rejected and spat out, are determined wholly by the child's individual inclinations. Such reactions involve the 'whole person' and are regarded as determined by the child as a total organism. Hence Rogers described these reactions as 'organismic'.

'Organismic' thoughts and feelings represent experience uncontaminated by parental values and the values of others. As we have seen, however, parents can transmit their account of experience, and this can lead to a child forsaking his or her own version and adopting the parental view.

The parents have the power to effect this change because a child needs such things as affection, approval, sympathy, respect and acceptance. These comprise what Rogers termed 'positive regard'. Since the child fears the loss of positive regard, he or she learns to interpret feelings and behave in ways that ensure that affection, attention, approval and so on continue to be given by the parents.

The child's fear of losing positive regard means that the parents can have a conditional relationship with the child. They can say, 'If you are obedient and kind, we approve of you and we will continue to be on good terms with you, but if you are disobedient or aggressive, we do not approve of you and you will lose the kind of relationship that you enjoy with us.' If the child's relationship with the parents is disrupted, he or she will work to re-establish it in order to regain positive regard. Where, incidentally, little or no positive regard is given, the child may become more and more preoccupied with how to gain it and will put more and more energy into its pursuit.

Positive regard and self-esteem are so inextricably linked with each other that Rogers regarded one as being synonymous with the other. The approval, respect and acceptance that parents communicate is turned into positive self-regard by the child. In other words the child internalises the positive regard of the parents: 'If my parents give me their approval when I am obedient, I should approve of myself. If they give me their disapproval when I am aggressive, I should disapprove of myself.'

If positive regard is conditional, the child will internalise this too: 'The conditions under which my parents give me their approval are the conditions under which I approve of myself.' Internalising positive regard and the conditions that go along with it result in what Rogers termed 'conditions of worth'. How much the child regards aspects of behaviour or personality as being of value will be determined by what value is placed on them by others. The child's dependence on others creates the possibility of being no longer true to his organism. True feelings can be disowned and the attitudes and values of others adopted.

The influences of positive regard, the circumstances in which it occurs and the resultant conditions of worth have their affect on the self-concept. For example, some children learn to suppress their aggressive feelings and exclude them from their self-concept. They do this for the sake of their self-esteem. Excluding aggressive feelings from the self-concept, however, creates certain problems.

Discrepancies between the self-image and organismic experience

It was stated earlier that the self-image must remain reasonably stable and unchanged since it is a reference point in the personality. From time to time, however, a person who has excluded aggressive feelings from the self-image may find him or herself in frustrating circumstances and aggressive impulses start to well up in the personality. Since these aggressive impulses communicate, 'You are not the person you think you are', they will be a threat and a person will develop ways of protecting the self-image. We can take note of how people describe their behaviour when they have behaved aggressively but do not wish to admit it – 'I was not being myself', 'They made me lose my temper' – and so on. These are clearly forms of words that protect the self-image.

The more that attitudes and feelings towards the self are false, the more the self-concept is a poor representation of a more authentic self. For the sake of explanation, let us call this authentic self 'the true self' and let us further suppose that this is an accurate representation of the kind of self portrayed in organismic experiences.

The more the self-concept differs from the true self, the more unrealistic it will be. Conversely the greater the overlap between the self-concept and true self, the more accurate the self-concept and the more integrated the personality. Using Figure 2.1 we can suggest various relations between the self-image and the true self. We can say that there are things a person believes about him or herself that are not true. This is an area of the self-image that is not covered by the true self. Second, there are beliefs a person has about him or herself that are true. This is the area where self-image and true self overlap. Third, there are things that are true about a person that he or she does not believe. This is the area of the true self that is not covered by the self-image. In terms of the example of aggression with which we have been working, it is out of this area of the true self that aggressive impulses arise to threaten the self-image.

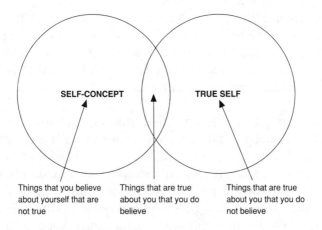

Figure 2.1 Truth and error in beliefs about the self

In this last instance, where impulses are arising from the true self to threaten the self-image, Rogers predicted that the self-image would become progressively more rigid and well defended. Thus threat can cause the continuance of an unrealistic self-image and prevent change.

Denial and distortion of experience

Experiences that are consistent with the self-concept are felt to be unproblematic. Experiences that are inconsistent with it are subject to denial and distortion – they either go unrecognised or are tailored to fit an already existent self-concept. People seek to ignore or redefine evidence that indicates that they might be someone other than the person they take themselves to be.

Let us look at an instance of how a person who had certain feelings was able to deny their existence. A nurse and doctor had begun to explain to the husband of a woman who was found to be terminally ill the serious nature of her condition. Seeing that he looked very angry, the nurse, wishing to give him an opportunity to talk about this, suggested, 'You must feel very frustrated and angry at what is happening to your wife.' This, however, the man denied.

Discussing the incident later both the nurse and the doctor agreed that he had given all the signs of being angry; his posture, his tone of voice and the expression on his face all indicated that he was very angry. They also found that both of them could not escape the impression that he did not know he was angry.

Subsequently they learned that this man had grown up in a family that adopted an extreme way of solving family conflict. When conflict arose between family members, such as his mother and father, they would simply stop speaking to each other. This period of mutual silence could last for a month or sometimes even longer. The overt expression of angry feelings in the family was never allowed or sanctioned. Not only did this feature of family history come to light but so also did the way in which this man had learned to become insensitive to anger in his personality. He continually looked at other processes at work in his personality and ignored his aggressive feelings. When the suggestion was made about just how angry he was, we could say that, instead of facing up to it, he looked in the opposite direction – he looked at what he thought of the doctor and nurse, or returned to what they had been talking about previously. He had reached the stage at which any angry feelings were given such minimum recognition that he could 'bristle with anger' without knowing it.

Denying experience in order to maintain a nonaggressive self-concept prevented him from facing up to how he felt about his wife's imminent death. Until he did this he could not start to adjust to the situation or begin the process of grieving for her.

The self-image and gender differences

Discrepancies between the self-image and the true self occur not only in individuals in unique ways but also on a wider scale as a result of general norms and values current in society. The differences in the accepted stereotypes of men and women is one such example.

Imagine a society in which one group of people, males, are regarded as independent and strong and allowed to experience some emotions, such as those involved in being assertive, competitive and adventurous, but are not allowed to experience others, such as those involved in being dependent, weak or afraid. The average man will seek to incorporate certain characteristics into his self-concept and exclude others. His self-concept will lead him to deny or distort awareness of any tendency to depend on others or of any weaknesses present in his personality.

If we accept that every human being will have to depend on others from time to time, particularly at times of personal crisis, and that every man will have a personality of which weaknesses are a part, then a man's self-image is bound occasionally to come under threat. If he is to retain his self-esteem, he will have to protect and defend his self-image. As we have seen, this will make it progressively more rigid and it will continue as an unrealistic representation of a more authentic self. He will be ignorant of the nature of his dependence and weaknesses while at the same time they will be continually there to threaten and undermine him.

Imagine a society in which another group of people, women, are regarded as dependent and weak and allowed to experience a wide range of emotions, such as those associated with being patient, affectionate and responsive to the emotional needs of others. Because society is accepting of her supposed dependence and weaknesses, the average woman can explore them. She can thus come to a realistic assessment of them and they can take their place in a self-image that reflects the realities of her personality. Her exploration of her weaknesses is in fact the road to psychological strength since it is not the suppression of weaknesses that leads to strength but a fuller understanding of them. Thus, in the kind of society we are imagining, women are likely to be psychologically stronger than men.

This is not meant to imply that women will be free from psychological problems. A woman, for example, who commits herself to the ideal of constantly fulfilling the emotional needs of every member of her family may be treating herself so badly that she eventually becomes emotionally exhausted and seriously depressed. This is particularly likely to happen if members of her family collude with her culturally defined self-image by taking what she offers without adequately rewarding her in return.

The ideal self

A person may not only persist with an unrealistic self-image but may also be hampered by an unrealistic ideal self. Again this can develop during childhood as the child imagines the kind of person he or she should most be like. The ideal self then becomes the self a person assumes he or she and others would value highly.

Again, using the example of aggression, a person may regard the ideal self as a nonaggressive one. He or she, at the same time, even though giving only minimum recognition to aggressive impulses, may be undermined by these impulses. Thus because of the way the ideal self is defined, there will be a lack of any healthy self-acceptance. This state of affairs then results in a low level of self-esteem. For this reason the greater the difference between the self-concept and the ideal self and the more unrealistic the ideal self, the more unhappy a person is likely to be.

The process of personality integration

A person who has an integrated personality is one who is not plagued by the consequences of conditional positive self-regard, the false values of others embodied in conditions of worth or an unrealistic ideal self. In such a human being there will be a high level of harmony between the real world, the self-concept and the ideal self. Where serious discrepancies between these three occur, there will be psychological disturbance and distress.

The key to an integrated personality is the discovery of the authentic meaning of experience in a climate that aids this process. If we take aggressive feelings in children as an example, what Rogers advocated was the freedom to explore aggressive feelings and genuinely to come to terms with them. A child's various impulses, feelings and behaviour, even if they are problematic, are matters that can safely be discussed and explored.

Enhancing this process is the acceptance of the child by parents. This acceptance is on the basis of recognising that the child is a human being and is therefore worthy of respect no matter what form individual thoughts or aspects of behaviour take. In other words the child feels of value in all conditions.

Rogers did not advocate a permissive attitude to the expression of feelings by children. Because acting on certain feelings can be destructive and can cause distress to other people, certain kinds of behaviour should be inhibited. However, inhibiting behaviour should not be accompanied by the denial of feelings and parents should recognise and acknowledge such feelings and indicate that they understand them.

Given the right conditions the authentic meaning of aggression can be sensed and discovered by the child, and, when this happens, its meaning will invariably take a constructive form. Aggressive impulses will ultimately be found lending their weight not to acts of destruction or cruelty but to protecting the weak, underprivileged or unjustly treated. Such protective actions will be expressed in a realistically assertive manner, spontaneously and without fear or inhibition.

3 MOTIVATIONAL PROCESSES AND CHILD DEVELOPMENT

SUMMARY

Maslow regarded psychological development as a personal need that depended on the fulfilment of other needs. These other needs were of four types. He put these in order and described how, when one type of need (low on his list) was satisfied, the next (higher on his list) made its appearance.

In addition to listing needs he also drew attention to the fact that the four needs on his list belong to one kind of motivation and the fifth, psychological development, to another kind. The distinction between these two kinds of motivation is related to another distinction made by more recent writers on motivation, that between rewarded behaviour and behaviour promoted by such things as interest and fascination.

The first half of this chapter will explain Maslow's theory of motivation and its implications for the development of a child and for life within his or her family. In the second half more recent work on motivation will be presented, particularly that concerned with the psychology of fascination. Also in the second half the implications of interest and fascination for child development and family life will be examined.

Introduction

Maslow (1968, 1970) combined an interest in motivation, mental health and development. His ideas on motivation and development and their implications for childhood experience are a major focus of this chapter and his ideas on mental health a major focus of the next.

In the present chapter we will consider first Maslow's description of differing needs and their operation. Then we will examine one of the areas of the study of motivation that has made considerable advances since Maslow's death in 1970. This area, which dovetails with his work and extends it, has been investigated principally by Csikszentmihayli (1975, 1992). It has come to be known as 'the psychology of optimal experience' but could well be described as the psychology of interest or fascination.

The nature of human motivation

Maslow believed that when one of a person's needs is satisfied, another appears to take its place. He also believed that fundamental needs could be listed in a way that indicated which need would appear when one lower in the list was satisfied. The fundamental or basic needs he identified were five in number (Figure 3.1). The satisfaction of the first type of need on the list leads to the appearance of the second type, and the satisfaction of the second to the appearance of the third and so on.

Type V Self-development

Type IV Self-respect and self-esteem

Type III Belonging and love

Type II Safety and security

Type I Physiological needs

Figure 3.1 Maslow's hierarchy of needs

If we go through this list, we can see that when an individual's physiological needs, such as the needs for food and drink, have been satisfied, he or she will seek to gratify desires for safety and security. Once, however, these desires have been gratified, needs fulfilled in satisfactory relationships emerge, such as those for love, attention and belongingness. If these are in turn gratified, the need for self-respect and self-esteem becomes prominent. Finally, following the satisfaction of these needs, a set of motives appears that is intimately concerned with psychological growth and the development of one's talents, a process known as 'self-actualisation'. At the highest level of motivation a person will also have a desire for such things as truth, beauty, wholeness and meaningfulness (Maslow, 1973).

We can give an example of each kind of need in Maslow's list as we imagine a person moving from one need to another. As a person does this, we can see how a motive or desire, present at one point in time, assumes the satisfaction of a more basic one and a lack of interest in a more advanced one. For a person who is dying of hunger or thirst, other needs will be trivial. There will not be any interest in the need for safety and security. If he or she is not experiencing physical needs but is living in circumstances that are threatening or unpredictable, the need for safety and security becomes paramount and the satisfaction of needs such as those for love and affection will not figure as priorities. However, if those needs satisfied in wholesome relationships are being fulfilled but he or she suffers from a prevailing sense of helplessness and inferiority, the process of psychological growth and development will not be taking place. Finally, if a person is to a marked extent working at what that person is uniquely fitted for and has a lively curiosity in the world around him or her, we can assume that the needs for self-respect and self-esteem have been satisfied.

A contrast between different types of need

Maslow distinguished between the first four types of need and the fifth. The first four arise from a deficiency or lack that directs or drives a person to seek gratification. These Maslow designated 'deficiency-needs' or 'D-needs'. By contrast the fifth set of needs is centrally concerned with a person's psychological development. Consequently they are designated 'being-needs' or 'B-needs'. They operate in quite a different way from D-needs. They do not derive from a lack nor do they disappear once they have been fulfilled.

The satisfaction of a D-need will generally be of relatively brief duration, will often involve a climax of some sort and will be followed by a new form of discontent. Also a D-need which is frequently fulfilled will be one which is taken for granted and undervalued.

B-needs, on the other hand, tend to be continuously present in an individual and are self-motivating. B-needs were regarded by Maslow as being weaker than D-needs. They could easily fade away in response to unrealistic attitudes and entrenched habits. A person whose principal aim in life is to 'eat, drink and be merry' may not acknowledge any need for personal development. However, he or she may, from time to time, feel unfulfilled, vaguely dissatisfied and unhappy.

Comparing the effects of satisfied and unsatisfied needs

Of course, needs lower in Maslow's prioritised list or 'hierarchy' are those which for the majority of people in our society are regularly satisfied. In terms of progressing from one level of need to another, problems are most likely to arise not at the lower levels but at that point at which other people are necessary for the supply of such things as love, attention or approval. Because these needs, which are satisfied only in relationships, may not be adequately met, many people are prevented from moving on to the highest level, which is concerned with psychological development and growth. The curbing of development in this way has a number of serious psychological implications, which we will now examine by comparing one person who had her needs met with another who did not.

Two teachers who taught in different schools were discussing the problems presented for one of them by a girl in her mid-teens. During the course of this conversation it emerged that the other teacher taught her identical twin sister. (The mother of these sisters had died at their birth and they were subsequently brought up separately by two distinctly different branches of the family.) Although what follows simplifies their separate childhood histories, it does illustrate important features of Maslow's theory. As far as the teachers could discern, the needs of one of the twins, who did not manifest the problems her sister had and who could be described as developing well, had been continually satisfied. This child grew up in relatively ideal circumstances. As a result of her needs being met, she learned to exploit her potential so that, as she approached adulthood, she had an identity that reflected the capacities with which she started life. She was self-assured and was maturing intellectually, socially and emotionally.

The second twin, who posed various problems, grew up under less than ideal circumstances and some of her needs were not met. It was clear from the way she behaved that amongst these was her need for attention. Because she did not receive even very minimum amounts of attention, she became preoccupied with searching for it. Pursuing her desire for attention led to the neglect of her psychological development. As Maslow (1968) showed, this problem was associated with others.

First, the need for attention will affect identity. We can envisage this teenager starting out on life with the same potential as her twin sister (Figure 3.2), which, like her sister, could have developed into a unique personality. Now instead of this, what has formed is the personality of an attention seeker. This is an identity that does not represent her initial potential.

The problems the second twin has in relation to her identity are sometimes exemplified in difficulties she has in decision making. When she was a child, you could have asked her, 'What do you want to do today?' This question is not easy to answer because what she wants is anything that will gain or hold your attention. This contrasts with the ease of decision making of the first twin, who is clear about her identity, clear about the kind of child or person she is, and is therefore aware of exactly what she wants.

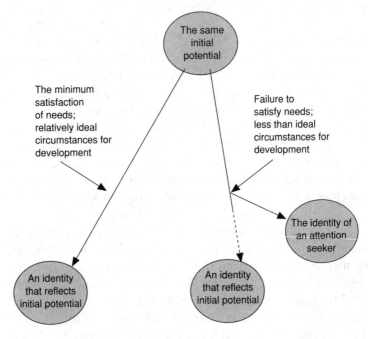

Figure 3.2 Identical twins developing differently

Second, because of her need for attention she will find herself under the control of others. When others withdraw the attention she needs, she must change her behaviour in order to regain their attention. Thus by giving or withdrawing attention others can produce changes in her behaviour, and, in a significant sense, it is they rather than she who influence her behaviour. She has lost the control that she should have and has become dependent on those who can dispense what she needs. She may not be fully aware of what is happening to her, but the very fact that others can 'call the tune' will make her feel vulnerable and frustrated and encourage her to view others with distrust, fear and hostility.

Third, even if the need for attention happens at this moment to be satisfied, a person who is attention seeking can never be sure that this state of affairs will continue. No matter how much attention she receives, she suspects that she will have to face its withdrawal in the future. The feeling that she cannot protect or insure herself against its withdrawal means that, even if others supply attention in relatively large amounts, she will not feel that her present sense of gratification can be relied on. Clearly those such as her teacher who spend time with her will face a dilemma: if they do not give the attention she craves, she pesters them for it; if they do give it, it is never enough and she always seeks more.

Fourth, this need for attention will affect the way she views other people. It will result in a marked tendency to look at others solely in terms of whether they satisfy her need for attention or not. She will not appreciate others in terms of their own unique characteristics, but will rather see them only as potential sources of supply. Even when socially engaged with those who supply attention, she will not take into account what they are really like as people. She will not adequately accommodate her reactions to theirs or take into account their own personalities since her only concern is capturing their attention. Her ignorance of what they are really like and her lack of interest in them result in her talking 'at' them rather than 'to' them. Obviously this does not encourage their interest or maintain the supply of attention that she needs. When they are with her for any length of time, they are manipulated into listening to her and find themselves drained because she is so unrewarding to be with.

The problematic experience of the twin who has lacked attention can be contrasted with the other twin who had her needs, including her need for attention, satisfied so that she has been able to move on to satisfying other needs, including that of self-development. As a result her identity is an accurate one.

The potential that resided in her at birth is being exploited so that her feelings, thoughts and behaviour and her identity represent the person she is.

It also follows from this that, knowing who she is, she will be governed by her own intrinsic nature and, unlike a dependent person, will be in control of her own behaviour. She will not be oversen: 'ive to the attention and goodwill of others. Paradoxically because others, especially those who took responsibility for her upbringing, have adequately satisfied her needs in the past, she is less dependent on them (and others) and feels less negative or ambivalent about them. Furthermore, her perception and feelings for people will be based not on the use she can make of them but rather on the qualities they possess. Since she is motivated progressively more by her being-needs, she finds each step in personal growth, whether in school or other settings, satisfying and fulfilling.

The satisfaction of needs in the family and personal crisis

Since most social needs are satisfied in a person's family, the family could be described as a system that produces love, attention, approval, respect and so on at a certain level and distributes them amongst its members, although not always evenly. This may seem a rather mechanistic view of family functioning but it provides a useful way of assessing what might be described as the psychological health of the family and its morale. It also provides a useful way of analysing the difficulties that arise when certain changes take place in a child's life which result in a change in the levels of love, attention, approval and respect that he or she receives from family members. Let us take the transition from home to school as an example.

Before a child goes to school he or she can behave dependently in ways that satisfy certain social needs. For example, assuming the mother is the major caretaker, her attention can often be gained at will. A child can also behave relatively independently, choosing to play for various periods of time without losing the approval or respect of the parents. In fact a parent may respond to these periods of independent play with approval.

When a child goes to school, however, he or she must submit to a different set of rules about dependence and independence, and these will affect the supply of attention and approval. In the school setting it is not always possible or appropriate for the child to gain the teacher's attention at will, nor can he or she behave independently in the same way as at home. Not only this, but the regular supply of needs that a child has become accustomed to at home will disappear when first going to school and must be re-established in this new setting. To this problem may be added the more obvious problem of a child facing a deliberate withdrawal of approval and affection by the parents if he or she does not adequately adjust to school life or even refuses to go.

Paradoxically the more intimate and wholesome a child's relationship with his or her mother or major caretaker, the more difficult this transition may be. Such a transition may represent a crisis for the child since, as some writers suggest, a central feature of many crises is 'a loss or threat of loss of basic psychological supplies' (Caplan, 1964, p. 35).

In adult life there is incidentally no better example of this feature of a crisis than bereavement, a circumstance in which the needs satisfied by (say) a marriage partner over perhaps a large number of years suddenly cease to be fulfilled. Following on from what has been pointed out about family functioning, the quality of social support available to a person, through which others offer new sources of affection, respect and so on, is directly related to recovering from a crisis such as bereavement (Marris, 1986; Parry, 1990).

Self-perpetuating motivation

The distinction that Maslow made between D-needs and B-needs is one which is mirrored in another distinction made by writers in this area, that between extrinsic and intrinsic motivation. The kind of motivation that promotes an activity by means of rewards is referred to as 'extrinsic'. Clearly D-needs operate on this basis. Contrasting with this kind of motivation is another that promotes an activity without relying on rewards. This is described as 'intrinsic' and includes such psychological processes as interest and fascination. In childhood and usually in adulthood, play when it is done non-competitively and for enjoyment is an intrinsically motivated activity. B-needs are also an example of this kind of motivation.

As both the first half of this chapter and a large part of behaviourism (see Chapters 9–12) is concerned with explaining how extrinsic rewards operate, we will look now at a form of intrinsic motivation that is important for development. It is a form which extends our understanding of how the exploitation of a person's potential takes place.

Csikszentmihayli (1975, 1992) has studied a set of psychological processes that combine both intrinsic motivation and personal development. These processes are each a part of what he has called 'flow,' which is an experience that occurs when a person is completely immersed in a task. He defines this as 'the holistic sensation that people feel when they act with total involvement' (Csikszentmihayli, 1975, p. 36) and he has studied this experience in a whole range of activities, including basketball, composing music, dancing, performing surgery, rock climbing and playing chess. These studies have had adult experience as their major focus, but clearly the processes that have been discovered apply equally to childhood. Being 'in flow' has the following features.

1. In doing the task the individual's mind and conscious awareness become narrowly focused so that distracting or irrelevant thoughts or perceptions are eliminated. He or she is wholly concentrating on the task and is fully involved and participating in it.

   You can imagine a rock climber, for example, fully occupied with the rock face and with considerations of how to conduct the next stage of the climb. Danger may aid in 'concentrating the mind' but, once sustained attention has begun, danger may no longer be influential or even noticed.

For the chess player 'in flow', the rules of the game become the channel along which the mind travels to the exclusion of all other stimuli. For the duration of the game all other concerns are excluded.

2. The task that produces flow is one that is matched to a person's ability to perform it. It must be neither undemanding, in which case boredom may result, nor too demanding, in which case worry or stress may result. Incidentally, Csikszentmihayli's first book (Csikszentmihayli, 1975) was entitled *Beyond Boredom and Anxiety*; it might have been more appropriately entitled **Between** *Boredom and Anxiety*.

Rock climbers who experience flow match their skill to a physical obstacle. Their level of competence is perfectly engaged by the demands of the rock face. For this reason the climb must not be too easy or difficult. An easy climb will not produce the right level of challenge and could result in boredom. Alternatively a climb that presents too much difficulty will produce psychological states varying from worry to acute anxiety.

Chess players struggle against internal obstacles. Challenge occurs in the form of intellectual demands. Intellectual skills are matched to the mental problems posed by the game.

Since a person who is absorbed in doing a task or is fascinated by it will be doing it over and over again, he or she is likely to become progressively better at it. A task that was once difficult will then become easy (and therefore boring) and will no longer offer a matching of ability to the performance required. For this reason a task regularly associated with flow must be one that can offer different levels of difficulty so that with increasing proficiency a person can move on to a more challenging level.

Rock faces for an enthusiastic climber must become progressively more difficult since the climber's ability continually improves with practice. Similarly the chess player must take on increasingly more expert players who offer more demanding challenges.

When the level of stimulation is right a person is functioning according to his or her own sensory, physical and intellectual capacities, a process that sustains the activity in spite of the lack of explicit rewards. This pleasure contrasts with that deriving from achievement. In the process of flow, achievement itself is not a major source of satisfaction. What is really important is the fact that during the activity boredom and anxiety are avoided.

3. While working on the task, the person obtains clear understandable feedback; that is, the feedback presents consistent demands, demands that do not need clarifying or sorting out. A person knows how well or badly he or she is doing.

   Although achievement does give some feedback in the form of an indication of performance, achievement is not in itself, as we have seen, a major characteristic of the flow experience.

4. As a result of points 1, 2 and 3, action fully occupies awareness. Fully engaged in the task, performers are aware of their actions and what is happening but are not aware of their awareness. In other words they become unself-conscious. The climber and the chess player merge into their respective activities and perform them totally unself-consciously.

5. With the sense of challenge, matching abilities to the task in hand, comes a sense of novelty. What appears to occur is that the task the person has undertaken allows him or her to use physical and mental potential in a novel and challenging way and to have new experiences at the boundaries of freshly developing ability. This leads to a sense of discovery and exploration.

The sense of novelty may be so strong that the experience of flow takes on a quality different from the mundane, everyday world. The climber and the chess player again illustrate this. They explore and expand their abilities while at the same time feel that they are inhabiting 'another world' or a 'strange place'.

6. The flow experience brings with it a sense of freedom. A person fulfils his or her desire to be a cause and with this comes an increased sense of control over the immediate environment.

7. The flow experience is associated with personal development. The person is finding out, through receiving an optimal level of stimulation, the limits of personal abilities, and, in overcoming these limits, is engaged in a process of personal discovery. Again, climbers illustrate this. They sometimes describe their experience of flow as a form of self-communication.

These seven characteristics can more often than not be related to each other and are dependent on each other. For example, screening out all distractions (1) leads to exploration and discovery (3) and an increased level of control (6); the simplicity of feedback (3) aids in screening out distractions (1) and helps a person to become unself-conscious and lose self-awareness (4); and the challenges (2) and feedback (3) are perceived with complete clarity so that the task can be managed in a way that gives a sense of freedom (6).

Some features of flow combine in their effects to produce further characteristics. Screening out irrelevant perceptions and thoughts (1) and losing self-awareness by merging into the activity (4) result, for the duration of flow, in a release from ordinary, everyday difficulties and problems and those worries and concerns that a person has about his or her identity. Thus flow may represent a welcome period of relief from the recurrent problems of life. For the rock climber and chess player, their respective activities are experienced as completely separate from normal life.

Obviously flow experiences will occur in some people more than in others. It is also true that certain tasks are in themselves more likely to produce this experience. Hence the kind of person you are and the kind of activity you are engaged in act in conjunction. For example, you may be the kind of person who needs less or more of the structure provided by the rules in a game like chess.

The family as a context for flow

We can draw an analogy between the kinds of activity described above, such as chess, and a child's life within a family. When playing chess gives rise to the experience of flow, the rules of the game are in the background. The rules direct attention but are not in themselves the focus of attention. They leave a person's mind wholly free to concentrate on the task in hand. Thus the chess player in flow has every part of his or her attention available for the events of the game.

The rules and structure of family life can be seen in the same light as those of chess. Some families will have a lifestyle or rules that provide a context in which a child can easily engage in the 'flow' of whatever activities he or she chooses – be it free play, a conversation or a game. Other families will create an atmosphere in which the rules are so unclear or inconsistently applied that they have to be constantly attended to and interpreted. This kind of family operates like a game of chess where the rules are not agreed, and therefore the rules, and not the playing of the game, become a disrupting focus of attention.

As the study of flow has aptly demonstrated, the development of any ability or talent can only occur with a distinctive kind of involvement in a particular context. In the case of a child, Piaget (1954) envisaged this involvement and the development it fosters in the following way. Because a child cannot cope with the same range of stimulation as an adult, much of the surrounding world is ignored. However, there will be an aspect of the world or, more specifically, a form of stimulation and activity that catches the child's interest and attention. To choose a simplistic example, a child is, at a certain stage, fascinated by the problem of building a wall with wooden blocks. This will be a form of stimulation and activity that fully engages the child's interest. But it will be one which he or she can only partially cope with. The child has difficulty placing one block on top of another and next to others to form a wall.

By involvement and practice, the child gains mastery. What happens then is that another perhaps more advanced or more complex form of stimulation challenges the child. The child attempts to build a tower with the blocks. This form is again an aspect of the environment that catches the child's interest and attention, but again it is one over which he or she has only partial mastery – shown by the fact that the tower is not very high before it falls down. With time and practice mastery is again achieved, with the result that yet another aspect of the environment presents a challenge. Piaget envisaged this cycle of events being repeated over and over again so that the child learns to adjust to and deal with increasingly complex aspects of the world.

Each of the features of flow identified can be regarded as a pointer to the kind of context that gives a child the freedom to engage with whatever form of stimulation is attracting his or her attention. Such freedom grows out of living in a family that has the characteristics that conform to what we already know about flow.

1. The family provides a supportive context for those occasions when the child is attracted to a particular mental or physical activity that takes up all of the child's concentration. The activity itself, and not the rewards or consequences that it may produce, becomes wholly the focus of attention. Attention given to rewards and consequences distracts and disrupts the enjoyment of the intrinsically motivated activity that is promoting the child's development.

2. For the child the rules of family life should not be undemanding, in which case boredom will result, or overdemanding, in which case anxiety will result. The family will be supportive of, perhaps even committed to, the child's involvement in activities at the level of his or her abilities.
3. The clarity of the rules and norms of family life make possible the child's focus on the feedback that comes from the intrinsically motivated activity in which he or she is engaged. The family does not create any unnecessary obstacles to receiving feedback.
4. There are no difficulties posed by family members that inhibit the child's unself-conscious involvement in activities that produce flow.
5. The child has the freedom to develop, which means moving in what, for the child, is a novel direction. This is the freedom that is epitomised in play.
6. Freedom of choice (5) enhances a sense of control.
7. The child's natural absorption in those activities that promote psychological growth and development can carry on in an uninhibited way. The family can enhance the sense of exploration and enjoyment that is normally experienced in playful activities.

Ideally parents will create an atmosphere in which they are sufficiently sensitive to the child's experience that all the factors promoting flow are in balance. Since context is important because it provides rules that direct activity, children must not be left completely to their own devices. On the other hand parents must not interfere too readily in the processes involved in flow since such interference can be disruptive and coercive. The best challenges are those that capture the child's attention rather than ones that are being imposed.

An analysis of the developmental processes involved in flow may make the process appear more complicated than it usually is in practice. For example, observations of the transactions between various family members will demonstrate that grand-parents have conversations with their grandchildren and assist them in activities in which both parties become deeply inter-ested and fully engaged.

Rathunde (1988), who developed ways of analysing back-ground factors in family life that are associated with flow, showed that such factors could be measured and investigated. He found that those adolescents who saw the context of their family life as having the features described above experienced flow more readily at home. The advantages of home carried over to school, where these adolescents also experienced flow more easily and benefitted from it.

Satisfying a child's needs and overindulgence

The satisfaction of a child's needs and the promotion of a child's engagement in flow should not, incidentally, be confused with parental indulgence. Maslow saw submitting to discipline as a natural outcome of adjusting to the world. In order to fully exploit his or her potential, a person must recog-nise the necessity of submitting to the discipline of hard work.

Not only may a child learn the need for discipline in the process of his or her development, but the world in which he or she lives may also teach this lesson. Neither the physical nor the social world yields to a person's whim, and in order to be realistic a child must learn this. In the social world the child cannot or should not gratify his or her needs without reference to the needs of others. Although a minimum level of fulfilment of personal needs is essential, Maslow regarded unbridled grat-ification as dangerous. As the child learns to recognise the needs of others and matures, such things as impulses and feel-ings will become subject to delay, tolerance and control.

4 PSYCHOLOGICAL DEVELOPMENT AND PSYCHOLOGICAL HEALTH

SUMMARY

For humanistic psychologists the psychological development of a person, the exploitation of his or her potential, is synonymous with progress towards a mentally healthy state. Both Rogers and Maslow were interested in defining the nature of this state and identifying its attributes. Rogers' views are explained in the first half of this chapter and Maslow's in the second.

In order to contrast the condition of mental health with some of the problems posed by mental immaturity, psychological processes at work in each of these two states will be explained.

Introduction

The concepts of psychological growth or development and good mental health have a central place in the thinking of humanistic psychologists. Both Carl Rogers (1961) and Abraham Maslow (1970, 1973) described attributes of the fully developed and mentally healthy person that they had discovered in the course of their work. They also described those processes that inhibit or facilitate progress towards development and health. In examining this subject we will look first at the ideas of Carl Rogers and then at those of Abraham Maslow. Their ideas are complementary and overlapping.

This chapter aims not only to describe the components of mental health but also to explain how they work. This will be done by comparing the psychology of healthy with that of less healthy individuals. Taking this approach, particularly with respect to Maslow, we will be looking at only a small sample of the many components that have been identified.

Rogers' view of mental health

Rogers believed that there was one common motivational force that is present in all living things: all living things are motivated to realise their own potential. This making actual what is potential, sometimes referred to as an 'actualising' tendency, is seen in human beings. Each person acts to develop and then maintain all aspects of his or her being.

In early life this kind of motivation underlies an almost inevitable pattern of maintenance and progress. It can be seen in basic biological processes such as breathing, which is essential for a person's continuing existence and is a force that is irresistible, as holding one's breath for any length of time demonstrates. This 'actualising' tendency can also be seen in the development of various skills such as walking. Learning to walk, like many of the struggles necessary to make progress, again demonstrates a force that is strong enough to overcome initial failure and frustration.

With the development of the sense of self, the individual's motive for 'self'-actualisation appears. This will be a lifelong process in which an individual's aim is to exploit and realise inherently unique characteristics and capacities, becoming the kind of person initially implied in his or her potential. This process of self-actualisation is brought about by social rather than biological processes.

Self-actualisation is regarded as the same as becoming progressively more mentally healthy. Rogers described it as an ongoing process; the healthy person is not so much in a certain condition or state as being caught up in one psychological change after another. Positive mental health is not 'a destination, but a direction' (Rogers, 1961, p. 186). This direction does not guarantee continual happiness since, as we have seen in the example of learning to walk, it sometimes involves struggle and pain. It means having the 'courage to be' and 'launching oneself fully into the stream of life' (Rogers, 1961, p. 196).

Rogers recognised several characteristics of mental health. Four will be examined here. These are an openness to experience, living fully in each moment, trust in one's whole being and a sense of freedom.

Openness to experience

Experience, for Rogers, is everything that is taking place in the individual, and although a person is aware of only a portion of this, he or she is potentially capable of becoming aware of most of it. There are, however, processes at work in the personality which prevent openness to experience. These deny or misinterpret the truth of experience. To explain how this happens, we will look at the influence a person's self-image has on the way in which psychological processes and the outside world are perceived.

Central to Rogers' view of how the personality functions is the self-image or self-concept. Because this is the most important reference point in the personality, psychological steps are taken to keep it stable and consistent. Thoughts and feelings originating within a person or events occurring outside him or her will sometimes be interpreted in ways that deny or distort their reality if they are out of step with the assumed picture of self. Such denial or distortion can protect the self-image by reducing or eliminating the anxiety-producing threats that arise from any indications that an individual is not the person he or she assumes.

One way of explaining how experience can be denied or distorted and structured according to certain preconceptions is to examine a set of processes that psychologists and sociologists (e.g. Berger, 1966) have referred to as 'selective perception'. Selective perception is particularly likely to occur in people who are so strongly committed to a set of ideas that they are prejudiced.

If a person has a prejudice against any group of people – men, women, a racial or religious group – he or she will have a mental picture or stereotype of what a person belonging to that group is like. This picture is usually learned or picked up not from contact with members of the group against which a person is prejudiced but from people such as parents and teachers.

Let us take the example of a man who is prejudiced against a racial group, black people, and look at what happens when he encounters one. When they first meet up, he will be sensitive to any features that are part of his mental picture of what a black person is like. Being sensitive to some things, he is insensitive to or ignores others. What occupies his awareness is what fits his preconceived beliefs. What does not occupy his awareness are those features of this particular person that are out of step with what he expects to find.

If, for example, he assumes that black people have 'a chip on their shoulder' and are bigoted, he will interpret anything that is said forcefully or with conviction – however little this may be – as being in obvious agreement with what he anticipates and as representative of what black people are like. Any liberal views that are expressed will have no impact – they will go unrecognised and be ignored. It is as if, without being aware of it, this prejudiced person sifts the information that is presented to him. As a result the more times he meets a black person, the more convinced he becomes that he knows what this person is like, and this is so even if his original picture is a fairly inaccurate one. Certain preconceptions are organising what he sees and hears so that certain interpretations of what is taking place emerge no matter how out of step they are with reality.

A person's self-image can become a form of selective perception and can operate in the same way as this man's prejudicial stereotype. Strong commitment to a certain self-image can lead to sifting and misinterpreting the information of experience. Using the guide of the self-image, the thoughts and feelings that are occurring within a person and the situations of which he or she is a part can be denied and distorted. The way they are interpreted is in line with the preconceptions that the individual has about him or herself.

Openness to experience involves a freedom from such denial, distortion and misinterpretation. It involves, as far as is possible, awareness of thoughts and feelings without preconceived notions being imposed on them. Openness to experience means that the individual has conscious, uninhibited access to all that is going on within him or her. Such openness, apart from putting a person in touch with the truth of experience, will also lead to the creation of a more realistic self-image and clearer identity. The self-image will become an accurate representation of who the person is.

All three characteristics − accessibility of inner processes to consciousness, correctness of the self-image and clarity of identity − have been used as criteria of mental health (Jahoda, 1958). They describe the individual whose personality processes are in harmony with the true meaning of experience or, to use Rogers' term, 'congruent' (see Chapter 1).

Living fully in each moment

The second characteristic of mental health involves living fully in each moment. If a person does this, is open to experience and is therefore free from selective perception, each moment will have a unique quality. This is because a person is constantly learning from experience and changing. At each moment, as a changed and different human being, he or she appreciates familiar (and unfamiliar) situations in a novel way. What is going on inside and outside the individual has never before existed in quite this combination.

Trust in one's whole being or organism

In Rogers' view 'organismic' experience is that which arises from the 'whole person' – not just the rational and intellectual but the emotional as well. When a person is responsive to a broad spectrum of information, he or she is well placed to see the self and situations of which the self is a part accurately and realistically.

The individual using the 'whole person' to sense what is happening will discover that this sensing provides a trustworthy and competent guide to thought and action. Total trust in the whole of one's personality or organism and openness to experience will result in all relevant information being considered, so that any judgements made and decisions taken are more likely to be valid.

A sense of freedom

The process of making judgements and decisions just referred to is enhanced when there is freedom from constraint and inhibition. When this is so, the individual will know he or she has the freedom to move in any of a number of directions. This freedom is related to another characteristic of mental health in which Rogers had an interest, the urge to create. Being free, an individual can take the best possible approach to his or her most important creation, the self, which represents potential made actual in a fully functioning person.

Maslow's view of mental health

Maslow designed a research programme to discover the characteristics of an advanced level of psychological development and mental health. The findings from this research programme led to the creation of his theory of motivation (described in Chapter 3). According to this theory mentally healthy people have had their basic needs satisfied – the needs for hunger and thirst, safety and security, love, attention and belongingness, and self-respect and self-esteem. They have then moved on to satisfying the need for self-development, which means exploiting and realising their potentialities, a process which Maslow, like Rogers, referred to as 'self-actualisation'.

In his book, *Motivation and Personality*, Maslow (1970) summarises the results of his research into mentally healthy people. When he first began his studies, he used two criteria to identify those who were significantly healthy and could be distinguished from average or psychologically unhealthy people. One criterion was the lack of the symptoms of mental disorder, and the other was evidence of the development of a person's capacities and talents. He also supplemented his research with the study of public and historical figures.

On the basis of his criteria, Maslow screened 3000 students. The results, however, proved rather disappointing. Only one student was found to fulfil Maslow's conception of a mentally healthy person and about another two dozen could be described as 'growing well'. Maslow drew two conclusions from these results. First, a significant measure of positive mental health may only develop in later life (say) after the age of 25. Second, his criteria were too strict to capture all but a few of the mentally healthy.

In spite of this disappointing result Maslow continued his research because he regarded the mentally healthy person as offering better insights into the fundamental character of human nature, especially in its most highly developed form, than those people whom psychologists customarily study, the average and the mentally disordered. He also thought that what he was learning from his studies could be used to improve a person's mental health. Indeed he suggested that therapy should not just concern itself with putting right what is wrong and returning a person to a normal state but should also aim to promote a mentally healthy condition that is above and beyond a person's ordinary, everyday functioning.

Maslow found a wide range of differences that distinguished the healthy from the unhealthy. By way of example we will review a number of these.

An unbiased perception of reality

Maslow found that a mentally healthy person was more accurate or more 'efficient' in his or her perception of reality than the less healthy. The exact nature of reality is often difficult to define, especially where people and social events are concerned. For example, it is extremely difficult to assess just how obstinate a person is or how interesting a conversation happens to be. Nevertheless Maslow was able to identify those sources of bias that cloud the judgement of the unhealthy. Such sources of bias include anxiety, fear, need, desire and wish. Let us look at how one of these operate in the less than healthy individual.

Laing (1969) gives a number of examples of how wish may bias perception and cause problematic and unhealthy attitudes. Suppose that a man who is sexually inexperienced embarks on a marriage with high expectations of the sexual satisfaction it will bring. Let us further suppose that the sexual side of his relationship with his wife leaves him dissatisfied. The enjoyment he imagined before he was married is not being realised.

He can deal with this problem in three different ways. The most unpleasant from his point of view would be to attribute the origins of his dissatisfaction to himself – his incomplete sense of sexual pleasure may derive from his inability to relate to his wife in a sufficiently sensitive or virile manner. A second and perhaps for him less unpleasant way of perceiving his problem would be to regard the fault as lying in his wife – she does not relate to him in a sufficiently attractive or seductive manner.

A third way of dealing with the problem is to misinterpret his experience; that is, he may imagine that everything that can be gained is being gained from the sexual side of their relationship. If he adjusts his standards in this way, he will not have to face the unpleasantness of finding himself or his wife at fault. His wish to avoid the problem biases his perception of it. Indeed his wish is closing the door to ever properly analysing what is wrong since a problem that is denied cannot be examined or resolved.

What makes this process of perceiving reality in the light of certain wishes easier than may at first appear is that it is possible to react to any psychological discomfort or anxiety before it is properly recognised in consciousness. A person may react to a vague, undefined sense of unease by producing a comforting interpretation. He or she may come to do this with respect to not just one area of life, such as sexual dissatisfaction, but also others. This means that it has become a well-practised habit tantamount to an automatic response. Furthermore, a person is likely to rely on others to collude in these acts of self-deceit. For example, this man may have a wife who is also sexually dissatisfied, may also wish to avoid the unpleasantness of sorting it out and will therefore misinterpret her experience in a way that is in line with his view of what is taking place.

Those whose view of reality is biased by their wishes can also have a bad affect on the mental health of others and can eventually encourage them to adopt the same bad habit. Take, for example, a father who has always enjoyed telling his daughter what to do. He enjoys being domineering because this makes him feel important. As a consequence she is not allowed the kind of independence that other girls of her age have; he does not allow her to go out with her friends to late-night discos, parties and so on. When, however, she objects to her father's restrictions, he criticises her for being ungrateful. He says that he requires her to follow his advice because he has her best interests at heart and wishes to protect her.

Here is a father who has always enjoyed his position of authority over his daughter but interprets what he does in terms that imply affection and benevolence. This way of interpreting things fulfils another wish, his wish to see himself not as domineering (which he actually is) but as concerned about his daughter's welfare.

Difficulties arise for the daughter when her mother supports what her father says and there is a consensus in the family that the father is caring and benevolent. For a young child this consensus, which is not based on the realities of the situation, can be a serious source of confusion since she does not know whether to trust the feeling she has that her father is unjustifiably domineering or to trust what her father and mother are saying. In later life a child who has had this kind of personal history may be unsure about how to interpret her experience and therefore, like her father, becomes prone to interpreting it in line with her wishes.

Not only can perceptions of what is taking place be interpreted in the light of one's wishes but they may also be influenced by personality characteristics. One example given by Maslow was that of 'character-determined optimism or pessimism'. These are sources of bias that involve certain very fundamental aspects of a person's outlook that can lead to distorted judgement. Neither a very optimistic person nor a very pessimistic one is likely to perceive reality as it is. A social worker who views life pessimistically is likely to miss or fail to trade on the potential strengths of a client and his or her situation; alternatively an optimistic social worker may not fully acknowledge or come to terms with real and serious difficulties.

Because the healthy person perceives reality in an unbiased way, he or she can see the truth more clearly and is therefore better able to reason and draw valid conclusions. Mentally unhealthy people are not only unhealthy but, as can be seen from the examples above and as Maslow suggested, also are often wrong.

Realistic attitudes towards self

The sources of bias that Maslow identified affect all aspects of an individual's perception of reality, including the perception of the self. This aspect can also be misperceived because of a person's fears or desires. Wishing to perceive yourself as a certain kind of person or fearing that you may be a certain kind of person can prevent a more realistic perception or appraisal of self. In the same manner as indicated above in the example of a sexually unfulfilled man, a person may sense a threat to the self-image but not let this threat become clearly defined in consciousness. He or she then misperceives this experience and gives it an interpretation that perpetuates a false self-image.

The efficient way in which the mentally healthy person perceives the world and thinks about it includes the capacity to assess self realistically. Personal fallibilities and strengths are seen as they are and, because they are recognised as part of human nature, they are often accepted without undue worry or concern.

Because of being generally comfortable and relaxed about self, mentally healthy people are able to behave spontaneously without distorting or falsifying experience or hiding behind façades or roles. They are also less self-centred or egocentric than the average person. This makes them better problem solvers since they do not perceive what is going on around them in terms of how they would like to see it or in terms of how it may affect them.

Although the self-actualised person is generally accepting of self, he or she could not be described as complacent. Correctable personal weaknesses and failures do become matters of serious concern. Improvable shortcomings such as laziness and thoughtlessness over obstinate forms of immaturity, like prejudice and jealousy, do result in guilt and anxiety. The self-actualised person is opposed to these faults because they inhibit psychological growth.

A resistance to being influenced by the culture

In their outlook self-actualised people show what Maslow described as a resistance to 'enculturation'. Enculturation means 'being taken in' by one's culture. This happens because a culture can give a false meaning to a person's experience. We can look, for example, at the way in which common assumptions in the Western world have shaped the average person's experience of love. Both Erich Fromm (1962) and Rollo May (1972) have made a number of these assumptions explicit.

Fromm, in his book *The Art of Loving*, describes first how the average person experiences love as something that occurs easily and accidentally – a person 'falls' in love. It is something that happens to him or her over which there is little or no control. Second, love is largely caused or determined by the person who is loved. A man loves his wife because of the qualities that inspire his love. If, for example, she is beautiful, this will cause him to love her. Conversely if as she gets older she becomes less attractive or he starts to take her beauty for granted, she will no longer inspire his love and he will stop loving her. Third, in a market economy, love is affected by perceptions of reward and cost, profit and loss. When a man ventures into the marriage market, he is looking for the best possible deal. He knows what his assets are and wishes to marry someone who will offer assets equal to, and preferably greater than, his own. For example, many men and women have clear ideas about how physically attractive or otherwise they are and correspondingly know the kind of partner they are entitled to look for.

Love in our own culture and historical era has been described by May (1972, p. 9) in his book *Love and Will* as 'sentimental and experimental'. He suggests, by the use of the word 'sentimental', that men and women in our culture have been taught to experience their love as at the mercy of emotional whim. By the word 'experimental', he suggests that when men and women enter a loving relationship, they are like scientists conducting an experiment; the stance they adopt is that of a detached observer – without being committed or involved, they set aside any personal values and are simply looking to see what will happen.

Words such as 'love' and 'sentiment' go together in our own era. Words such as 'love' and 'will' do not. By contrast in previous historical eras, 'love' and 'will' sat comfortably together. In Christ's day, for example, he could command the disciples, 'Love one another', a command that could only make sense if loving was under the control of a person's will.

Now suppose that up to the age of 25 a man goes along with the way society defines love. As he gets older, however, and matures, he looks at his experience of love and finds it out of step with what society has taught him. He discovers that his developing humanity experiences love as a form of commitment, that his enjoyment of intimacy is accompanied by a sense of responsibility for the person loved and, as Fromm suggests, that loving is under the control of his will and he can work at it.

Mentally healthy people show a clear tendency to resist the values of the culture, especially where such values are inconsistent with their own developing humanity. In turn this resistance fosters a certain unconventionality. This is not a superficial form of rebellion sometimes seen amongst those who are adolescent or anti-authority. Rather it is an inner unconventionality that is based on the difference between the way in which society defines human nature and how human nature can be experienced by those who are mature. It is also based on the recognition that many of society's rules and norms are merely conventions and nothing more. In order not to be offensive to others, these conventions will often be observed, but at the same time there is a recognition that they are arbitrary rules rather than demands based on absolute truth.

Mental health and personal relationships

The mentally healthy person is much more autonomous than people in general who depend on others for the satisfactions that they cannot produce for themselves. For example, for most people friendship is based on the fulfilment of (say) the need for reassurance, support, love and so on. This kind of dependence on others leaves many people much more open to influence, manipulation and difficulties in making their mind up.

Self-actualised people on the other hand are dependent for their satisfactions on fulfilling the need for personal growth, the exploitation of their potential and latent abilities. They are therefore more independent of their social environment and less open to being influenced by it. Consistent with their autonomy is a distinct need for privacy.

Because of their independence of the social and physical environment, they are able to cope very much more easily with crises and deprivations. Since they are independent, they may sometimes be perceived as reserved and aloof or even unfriendly and snobbish.

In spite of their tendency to appear reserved, mentally healthy people are capable of much stronger relationships with their friends, showing, for example, a greater love, empathy, warmth and openness. They tend, however, to have few friends. This is not just because they value privacy but because intimacy of this intensity takes time to develop. Also those who have views similar to their own are very much in the minority.

Humour

Maslow found that the mentally healthy person's sense of humour differed from that of the average person's. What the latter finds funny often involves hostility, rebelliousness or superiority – apparent in jokes belittling members of minority groups or ridiculing certain forms of authority. In contrast, the self-actualised person's sense of humour tends to be what Maslow described as 'philosophical' (Maslow, 1970, p. 169). This kind of humour is often instructive, exposing, for example, some widespread hypocrisy or making fun of some other human weakness (although not making fun of human beings).

The capacity to appreciate the unique

No doubt the capacity a mentally healthy person has to perceive the world more realistically is related to his or her ability to appreciate what in situations and people is unique. In a manner reminiscent of selective perception, the average person categorises experience in the same way, day in and day out, and reduces much of it to mere repetition – another sunset is *just* another sunset, the journey to work is *just* another journey to work. Moreover objects and persons are judged and evaluated according to their utilitarian value.

The self-actualised person perceives objects and people without needing to evaluate their personal relevance. This involves care and attention, an acceptance of what is being perceived and a readiness to experience what is unique about an experience, be it a sunset or the relatively trivial journey to work. As a consequence perceptions do not lead to familiarity and boredom but to greater interest and a richer appreciation. This gives life an important sense of freshness. Life's experiences are enjoyed rather than taken for granted.

We can relate freshness of experience to the way in which the self-actualised person enjoys means as well as ends; that is, the doing of the task can be enjoyed as much or even more than the end result. In this 'means' behaviour, the mentally healthy person is likely to be more creative than the average person, showing the kind of creativity that is characteristic of the inventiveness and imagination of children.

Because of this tendency to appreciate and enjoy what is unique in experience, there are some things that the self-actualised person is less likely to see. He or she is unlikely to see or categorise people in terms of race, social class, political or religious groupings. The differences between people are enjoyed rather than being found to be threatening or intimidating.

An overarching purpose in life

Maslow found that his healthy subjects felt that they had a mission in life. This was something they not only wanted to do but felt that they had to do. Maslow thought that this attitude could well be necessary for achieving self-development. Self-actualised people were not interested in gaining money, fame or power but were involved in using their sense of mission to define who they were.

Related to this sense of mission is a deep-seated affection and empathy for human beings. Although mentally healthy people can be depressed and angry at human weakness and can be harsh with the hypocritical, pretentious, foolish and cruel, they tend also to be quick to understand and to forgive.

Also associated with their sense of mission is the fact that the healthy develop a highly ethical outlook. Their values grow out of an acceptance of their own nature and of human nature generally and a willingness to foster not only their own psychological growth but also that of others. As a result of this, they are not in any way confused or in conflict about what they regard as right and wrong.

Peak experiences

Finally Maslow found that some of the mentally healthy frequently had what he termed 'peak experiences'. These are moments or periods of awe and ecstasy. A person feels that self is being transcended and there is a sense of power, confidence and decisiveness and a feeling that there is nothing that a person cannot do or become. This experience may take on orgasmic proportions and may occur in response to such things as work, music or sex.

Not all self-actualisers were found to have peak experiences. These experiences occurred most frequently amongst those who were reflective and tended towards the mystical, the poetic and the religious. They tended not to occur amongst those who were more practical.

Other views of positive mental health

Although, as humanistic psychologists, Rogers and Maslow gave prominence to personal growth and positive mental health, they were not alone in the explanations they provided for this aspect of psychological functioning. Schultz (1977), for example, describes the models of mental health of seven theorists (including those of Rogers and Maslow). He points out that there is wide variation in the views of the different theorists but all are agreed on two attributes of health. First, mentally healthy people know who they are and, second, they are sufficiently autonomous to be in control of their lives.

SOME BASIC THEMES IN HUMANISTIC PSYCHOLOGY AND LINKS WITH THE INTRODUCTION

Basic themes in Part I

Not only can person-centred therapy be regarded as resolving the problems associated with certain ways in which the self-concept functions (Chapter 2), but it can also be the means of resolving the kind of motivational problems, such as attention seeking, that are examined in Chapter 3. Furthermore, insofar as person-centred therapy unearths more organismic experience and releases a person's humanity, it can be regarded as one possible route to the mentally healthy processes described in Chapter 4.

There are further important links between person-centred therapy, motivation and identity. Therapy facilitates a less inhibited approach to wishes and desires. This increases the clarity and validity of the self-concept. For example Csikszentmihayli (1992, p. 34) states, 'More than anything else a self represents the hierarchy of goals we build up bit by bit over the years.' In other words desires and the way in which they are organised constitute an important component of identity.

In Chapter 3 explicit links are made in Maslow's theory between motivation and personal development. Other links can however be made between the motivational processes described in Chapter 3 and the higher reaches of development and maturity described in Chapter 4. For example, there are many distinct parallels between Rogers' concept of the fully functioning person and what is happening to a person when he or she is in a state of flow.

In Chapter 1 reference is made sometimes explicitly and sometimes by implication to the qualities of a good therapist. The attributes of mental health that are reviewed in Chapter 4 have many connections with these desirable qualities. Rogers' description of openness to experience, which is central to his view of positive mental health, clearly relates to his concept of congruence. Also the kinds of relationship that self-actualised people value, the respect they have for other human beings and their highly developed ethical outlook, all attributes described by Maslow, relate to the respect and acceptance that underpins much of person-centred therapy.

Humanistic psychology and the change process

The general theory of change presented in the introduction suggested that when a problem is removed from one context to another, it is removed from those circumstances that support or maintain it. Person-centred counselling achieves this change of psychological context in a number of ways. First, any personal problems are likely to be examined entirely differently from the manner in which they have previously been examined. For example, the client experiences his or her problem being explored actively and sympathetically, as opposed to simply being given advice. Second, one of the most important things being confirmed in therapy is the client's reported experience. Independently of whether the meaning given to this experience is valid, the therapist communicates the recognition that this experience has occurred within the client and that its exploration can be the means of moving from the partial truths the client is caught up in towards a fuller, more complete understanding. Third, particular attention is paid to the feelings and emotions that, brought to the surface in a safe context, can guide and orient a person to efficient problem solving.

The client often puts the security of knowing who he or she is above the need to have a high level of self-esteem. Thus where clients as a result of processes such as confirmation and disconfirmation emerge from childhood with low self-esteem, they continually seek those experiences that confirm this low self-esteem because of the security this brings. By offering the conditions of acceptance and respect, the therapist provides a setting that creates a better balance between the need to have a *secure* sense of self and the need to change, develop and have a more *realistic* sense of self.

In line with Csikszentmihayli's concept of flow and Rogers' and Maslow's views on positive mental health, a person is better placed to know him or herself as an ongoing experience, that is, to be the *process* of self rather than holding on to the ideas that are perceived to be the *content* of self. Empathic understanding contributes to the discovery of this kind of self, and the therapist's genuineness, respect and acceptance to its emergence.

The historical and social context of humanistic psychology

Humanistic psychology has achieved its popularity coincidentally at a time when there has been an increasing emphasis in the Western world on individuality and personal growth. Unlike some of the more self-centred trends in the personal growth movement, it has not emphasised psychological growth at the expense of other people.

The expanding interest in counselling has also enhanced the popularity of humanistic psychology. Some have suggested that this has gone hand in hand in Western culture and particularly in the USA with the increasing failure of one person to listen to another. Counselling compensates for this failure.

FURTHER READING

On person-centered therapy and the self-image

1. Rogers, C.R. (1961) *On Becoming a Person: A Therapist's View of Psychotherapy.* Boston: Houghton Mifflin.

This book presents the major themes in Rogers' work from a number of different perspectives. Although it tends to be repetitive, it is usefully so.

2. Rogers, C.R. and Stevens, B. (1973) *Person to Person.* London: Souvenir Press.

In this book Rogers presents the principles on which his work has been based, and Stevens explores the ways in which these principles work out in experience.

All of Rogers' books are easy to read and have continued to be reprinted. They all discuss the therapeutic relationship and changes in the self from different perspectives. There are two further books that the reader may wish to consult. The first is Rogers' classic, *Client-centred Therapy* (originally published in 1951 by Houghton Mifflin) and the second is *Freedom to Learn for the Eighties* (published in 1983 by Charles Merrill), which details the implications of his ideas for education.

On motivation

1. Maslow, A.H. (1970) *Motivation and Personality.* London: Harper and Row.

In addition to covering Maslow's theory of motivation, this text contains a critique of psychoanalysis and behaviourism. It also has a number of chapters on self-actualisation and positive mental health.

2. Csikszentmihayli, M. (1992) *Flow: The Psychology of Happiness.* London: Rider.

This is an easy book to read summarising this area of motivation. Readers may also wish to read Csikszentmihayli's *Beyond Boredom and Anxiety* (published by Jossey-Bass in 1975) and a book of papers by several authors on a wide range of applications of the principles of flow, *Optimal Experience* (edited by M. Csikszentmihayli, and

I.S. Csikszentmihayli, and published by Cambridge University Press in 1988).

On positive mental health

1. Schultz, D. (1977) *Growth Psychology*. London: Van Nostrand.

This book summarises the work of Rogers and Maslow, along with that of five other authors. The classic text in this area, which is well worth reading, is Marie Jahoda's *Current Conceptions of Positive Mental Health* (published in 1958 by Basic Books).

PART II

INTRODUCTION TO PSYCHOANALYSIS

Freud (1856–1939) is rightly regarded as the founder of the psychoanalytic movement. Although there are several distinct psychoanalytic schools, they are all to some extent built on Freud's original interests and ideas. Three of his principal interests have continued to influence the psychoanalytic community: the nature of the unconscious, the search for the meaning underlying psychological processes and the role of personal history in the formation of personality and psychological problems.

The unconscious was envisaged by Freud as a world deep within the personality to which a person does not have direct access. It consists of instincts, impulses, feelings, wishes and ideas that act and react on each other. Because these processes are 'primitive, brutish, infantile, aggressive and sexual' (Ellenberger, 1957, p. 14), they are unacceptable, irrational and sometimes painful to any civilised person. For this reason they are kept from conscious awareness by another unconscious process – that of repression. Repression, however, is never wholly complete and the activities of the unconscious tend to express themselves in veiled form in daily life, for example, in dreams, slips of the tongue, jokes and so on.

Freud's belief in the unconscious originated from his relentless attempt to make sense of his patients' mental symptoms. These symptoms were either very poorly explained by the patients' rational statements or appeared to be meaningless. By postulating dynamic, unconscious processes, Freud found his patients' symptoms did, in fact, have meaning. Not only did symptoms have a hidden, underlying meaning but so also did the other aspects of ordinary life already referred to – dreams, slips of the tongue and jokes.

In addition to instincts, impulses, feelings and so on active in the unconscious, there are also certain childhood memories. These are relegated to the unconscious and repressed because of their unacceptable and painful nature. They play a part, however, in shaping a person's life. In the view of psychoanalysts the average person will not know or be aware of any of the most significant influences of the past on the present.

In the year of his death, 1939, Freud wrote a final formulation of his theory of personality (Freud, 1949), and it is on this that much of the fourth chapter in this section, Chapter 8, is based. To demonstrate how the components of Freud's theory work, we will look at a series of psychological processes known as defence mechanisms.

Freud's views are also in evidence in the first chapter in this section. This summarises the nature and progress of psychoanalytic therapy. In addition to Freud's views more recent practitioners using this kind of therapy are referred to. Freud's approach to therapy combined attempts at discerning what is happening at an unconscious level with elucidating the role played by the patient's early life in his or her psychological problems.

The second chapter in this section is designed to illustrate more fully the relation between personal history and psychological difficulties arising in the present. It relies heavily but not exclusively on the work of Karen Horney (1885–1952) and examines the subject of self-analysis. Horney belonged to a school of psychoanalytic thought that gave greater credence than did Freud to the influences of society and culture.

The third chapter examines first Freud's view of child development and then moves on to examine a contrasting psychoanalytical view, that of object relations theorists. These theorists regarded Freud's description of child development as being too concerned with later stages. He was particularly interested in the period between the ages of 4 and 7 years. The object relations group, however, assume that the first few months and years of life are of major importance. We will look at psychological differences between boys and girls to illustrate their theory.

5 PSYCHOANALYTIC THERAPY

SUMMARY

Because parents often act as 'authority figures', they create for their children a certain amount of anger and frustration. In later life when the child or adult relates to what he or she perceives as authority figures, the anger and frustration experienced with the parents can be revived and aspects of the parent–child relationship relived.

Where possible a person uses relationships in later life to examine and resolve problems arising from childhood experience. A psychoanalyst provides a context in which this is possible.

Like all adults, none of whom is free from the influence of the past, the therapist's own encounters with his or her parents have created emotional problems. Psychoanalysis is also therefore concerned with how the therapist's psychological problems can cloud the judgements that must be made in therapy.

Introduction

This chapter explains some general principles that guide analysts or therapists who have been schooled in the psychoanalytic method. Some of these principles were developed by Freud and can be regarded as traditional. Others are of more recent origin and exemplify the practice of analysts such as Casement (1985, 1990) and Fine (1973).

Psychoanalysis focuses on the influence of relationships in a person's early life, particularly parent–child relationships. Different psychoanalytic theories analyse these relationships in different ways. Contrasting ways of analysing childhood experience are presented in Chapter 7. What is presented in this chapter is an introduction to psychoanalytic therapy which covers general principles of practice without going into more detailed, theoretical perspectives.

The beginning of therapy

At the outset of therapy, the analyst explains the aim of treatment to the client. The client is informed that his or her psychological problems stem from processes at work in the personality which are outside awareness, that is, from unconscious processes. These can produce various symptoms, such as anxiety and depression. The aim of therapy is to gain access to unconscious processes and develop an understanding of their role in the production of symptoms. This understanding will then form the basis of change.

The means by which the therapist aims to study the client's unconscious is a method called 'free association'. This method, which originated with Freud, requires the client to allow thoughts to occur freely, to let the mind wander where it will and to verbalise everything, no matter how silly or ludicrous it may seem. The client may at first have some difficulty with this method, feeling too inhibited to share thoughts with absolute freedom. To reduce any inhibitions, he or she is asked to lie relaxed on a couch with the therapist sitting out of sight. After gaining some experience of free association, any unease usually quickly dissipates.

At various stages of therapy, the client will show what Freud described as 'resistance', an inability to talk about emotionally significant areas of experience. Such an inability can be regarded as a force separate from his or her will that manifests itself in hesitations and the flow of thought coming to an abrupt end. These manifestations provide the therapist with evidence of those areas of experience that pose particular problems for the client. In order to overcome resistance and enhance free association, the therapist will from time to time interpret what has been said.

The psychoanalytic view of what is wrong with the client

Jim commenced a course of psychoanalysis when he was in his early thirties. Some features of his early life provide material that can be used to illustrate important theoretical principles and ideas. As a boy Jim could well have been described as a very amenable child. He grew up in a family in which his father was a very dominant influence, and this influence naturally made itself felt in Jim's relationship with his father. Jim unquestioningly adopted a submissive role, and, with the passage of time, it became so habitual that he was not aware of the way in which he was responding to his father.

Not only did the father exercise a constant authoritarian influence but he also had a very strong affection for Jim. This affection made it very difficult for Jim to go against his father's wishes since he knew that any disobedience would result in his father's displeasure and a withdrawal of affection. On the rare occasions Jim did fall foul of his father's wishes, he found it very difficult to tolerate the consequent break in their relationship. Because of this and the condemnatory way in which his father interpreted Jim's occasional misdemeanours, disobedience (and eventually even the prospect of disobedience) resulted in strong feelings of anxiety and guilt.

Clearly there were times when Jim naturally and strongly desired to follow a course of action independent of his father's wishes. The father's dominance, however, continually crushed the boy's developing autonomy and became a potent source of frustration. This frustration was seldom expressed because of the ease with which Jim experienced guilt. Eventually he learned to keep his frustration totally in check. The more successful he was at this, the easier and more automatic it became. Eventually he was no longer aware of the fact that he was inhibiting his anger and frustration because it had become so natural to him.

Of course, as a child Jim was not able to describe or analyse what was happening to him. Apart from the fact that, like all children, he took much of his life for granted, he was also prevented from examining any possible faults his father might have had by the fact that he idealised his father. His father encouraged this. Habitually reigning back his frustration and continually idealising his father resulted in Jim being largely unconscious of the psychological problems his father had created for him. He was also largely unconscious of the link between his psychological problems and the symptoms he had, symptoms such as anxiety and occasional bouts of irrational anger.

The influence of past conflicts on the present

Conflicts are inherent in all parent–child relationships. Psychoanalysts suggest that insofar as parents are sources of emotional support, they inspire in the child affection and love, but insofar as they are sources of restriction, not allowing a child always to do what he or she sometimes strongly wishes to do, they will be sources of frustration and, possibly, hatred and hostility. Although from a purely logical point of view, it is impossible to love someone you hate or hate someone you love, human experience can simultaneously incorporate these emotions and generate a great deal of ambivalence.

Children's relationships with their parents may be seen as involving the same recurrent patterns of emotional support and restrictive demands. These patterns occur again and again throughout the years that are spent as a member of the family. Then, in using what they have learned from their relationships with their parents and applying it to other people, children will bring to these new relationships the specific emotional difficulties and problems that they experienced with their parents. The expectations derived from patterns of support and restriction in childhood are especially likely to be resurrected whenever the person becomes involved in a relationship later in life in which parallels can be drawn with the earlier parent–child relationship. Parallels are particularly likely to be drawn when authority and dependence are significant aspects of the relationship.

What is being described here in general terms is exemplified specifically and in detail in Jim's case. First, he learned to get on with or relate to a certain member of his family, his father, in a specific way. This way of relating was one which not only became natural, spontaneous and habitual but also generalised in its operation to others outside his family.

Second, the way he learned to relate to his father brought with it certain problems, and these problems were re-enacted whenever he behaved towards others as he had behaved towards his father. In other words the problems his father left him with also recurred in his relations with those he perceived to be in authority. Jim's natural drive towards independence had come to be inhibited, especially in his father's presence, and was also inhibited when with others whom he perceived to be authoritative. This problem was, as it were, 'written' into Jim's personality and the way he went about things. It operated beyond his awareness, at an unconscious level, and expressed itself covertly.

Although Jim was aware that something was wrong with some of his relationships, he could not come to grips with the real reasons for this and, as mentioned earlier, was sometimes anxious and inexplicably angry. Since Jim's wife was a person who had clear and decisive views, which she often put forward very strongly, Jim sometimes related to her as an authority figure, as someone like his father, and acted towards her in a submissive manner that was permeated with frustration. Not surprisingly she found it difficult to understand why he behaved like this.

The therapist regarded as a figure from the past

When a person embarks on psychoanalytic therapy, the therapist is likely to be seen as a person on whom the client is dependent and who is authoritative and takes control. Consequently this situation will trigger the emotional problems inherited from the parent–child relationship. The client, in a process known as 'transference', 'transfers' emotional reactions from (usually) parental figures in his or her past to the analyst. As we have seen this process occurs because the client, without realising it, assumes that there is a parallel between the parent (or some other significant person from the past) and the analyst.

Freud discovered the phenomenon of transference when he compared two kinds of experience he was having with his patients. On the one hand his patients reacted to him sometimes with inappropriate forms of aggression and sometimes with inappropriate forms of affection. On the other hand, having listened to what they said about their parents, he found that had he actually been one of their parents, his patients' reactions would have been justified. The unrealistic expectations that Freud's patients had of him clearly stemmed from the type of relationship they had had as children with their parents. His patients inadvertently 'transferred' to Freud what they had learned about their parents.

Transference may be either negative, involving the expression of frustration or aggression towards the therapist who is assumed to be (say) an unsympathetically demanding parent, or positive, involving expectancies consistent with (say) a caring, protecting parent. Therapy affords the opportunity to experience the range of feelings involved in both positive and negative transference. These extremes of feeling, because of the immature characteristics of the child and possibly the suppressive or intimidating atmosphere of the home, could not be examined or handled in early life.

Storr (1963) suggests that transference can be dramatically illustrated in two opposite types of client, the dependent and the autonomous. Dependent clients react to a therapist as if they always fear they will be abandoned. Because such clients seek to please, they react in ways that lead the therapist to overestimate progress. Imagine, for example, that a therapist is working with too cooperative a client and is thoroughly content with the apparent progress that is being made; the client is always very responsive to the comments, suggestions and interpretations that are being offered. However, on meeting the relatives of this client, the therapist may be surprised by the relatives' account of the client's failure to change or make any progress.

Not surprisingly there were many examples, particularly in the early stages of Jim's analysis, that were illustrative of the problems of dealing with a dependent client. Although he was not aware of the fact, particularly during the first few therapy sessions, he behaved as if one of his most important aims was to keep his analyst happy. Clearly he did this because it was often his intention to keep his father happy.

Autonomous clients, unlike the dependent, may fear domination by the therapist. They may continually express hostile feelings, often because they use the new found freedom that psychoanalysis provides to behave in ways that they would normally suppress. Their hostility, however, may lead the therapist to underestimate the progress they are making. After many unpleasant sessions with an independent and apparently cantankerous client, a therapist may be surprised to be told by his or her relatives of the marked changes for the better that are taking place.

Whether positive or negative, transference can be regarded as a specific example of a general tendency to make sense of the present in terms of the past. A new, evolving (and therefore unknown) relationship with the therapist provides an opportunity for the past to play a crucial role in forming the nature of the client–therapist relationship.

The influence of the therapist's past on the therapist's present

In psychoanalysis the therapist (rather like Jim's wife) is on the receiving end of transference reactions. This means that he or she represents a figure encountered earlier in the client's life who has been associated with certain unresolved feelings. Psychoanalysis is concerned with making sense of these feelings. However, therapists must not only try to understand the basis of clients' emotional reactions but must also deal with the problems posed by their own past. This past, like that of the client, biases perceptions of people and events and prevents such perceptions from being true to reality. The therapist, therefore, must cope with what is termed 'countertransference'.

Countertransference has been defined and explained in many different ways. We will look at two of these. First, let us look at an explanation that is in line with Freud's original formulation (Freud, 1910). This explanation suggests that countertransference is the influence of the client on the unconscious feelings of the analyst.

We can illustrate these processes by looking at the relationship between Jim and his therapist. At a certain stage in therapy, after some six sessions, Jim became anxious and agitated about what he saw as his lack of progress. He was anxious, not for his own sake, but because he feared what his analyst might make of this. His anxiety and agitation over his lack of progress communicated itself to his analyst, who was sorely tempted to calm him down and placate him. Her motives for doing this were based on her desire to prevent Jim from expressing high levels of anxiety. These motives were connected with her past as she had grown up in a family that could not tolerate or handle any strong or intense emotions and therefore encouraged their suppression. It is possible, of course, that, like her client, she was oblivious of how her experiences in her own family had influenced her and were driving her – to go to extreme lengths, if necessary – to keep her client calm.

We can see that if the analyst emerged from her early life with a deep-seated but unconscious need to prevent the expression of strong emotions, she may well aim to satisfy this need when she works with someone like Jim who needs to make her feel comfortable. There is here an unconscious communication taking place between Jim and his analyst. His need to make someone in authority feel comfortable makes contact with his analyst's similarly unconscious need to maintain everything on an emotionally even keel. The true dynamics of what is taking place are lost on both of them. This can result in no real progress being made. Analyst and client arrive at a psychological impasse that is a case of 'you scratch my neurotic back and I'll scratch yours'.

Incidentally Jim's analyst, had she reassured him, would have fallen foul of the psychoanalytic dictum, 'reassurance seldom reassures'. Generally blanket reassurance does not bring lasting (or sometimes even brief) relief because it leaves the client's problems unexamined and unresolved. People often give it not for the sake of the person in need but to provide some personal, although false, reassurance and comfort for themselves since their anxieties have been heightened by another's distress.

Some writers (Balint, 1952; Reich, 1951) have described countertransference not as the general influence of the client on the unconscious processes of the therapist but as a more specific process mirroring more directly the concept of transference. These writers suggest that the therapist, like the client, may unconsciously draw a parallel between the client's reactions and those that the therapist once received from a significant figure in his or her past. This leads the therapist to behave as if the client were actually this figure from the past.

Just as persons in the client's past can be associated with certain unresolved problems, so also can persons in the therapist's past. For example, Jim's therapist had in her childhood a wayward older sister who was occasionally cruel and destructive. The therapist inherited from her relationship with her sister an unresolved sense of helplessness in the face of another's uncontrolled and uncontrollable behaviour. At one stage in therapy, when Jim had moved from fearing and then idealising his analyst to denigrating and attacking her, she was tempted to respond, as she had in the past with her sister, by emotionally withdrawing and resorting to an unhelpful passivity.

Countertransference can be seen in more general terms than the two more detailed views we have looked at. It can be seen as any form of bias in the therapist that has its origins in the past. These must be recognised and analysed if he or she is to be of service to the client. Would-be therapists therefore undergo a lengthy period of analysis by a mature analyst so that in due course the trainee therapist can be informed of attitudes and behaviour that are the cause of unhelpful reactions to clients. Because the possible influence of such attitudes and behaviour requires sensitive monitoring, a trained analyst may from time to time seek periods of further analysis and supervision from another analyst.

Problems in interpretation

The therapist will wish to identify for the client patterns or trends in his or her past, the meaning they have and their influence on the present. However, transference and countertransference will make it difficult for the therapist to form accurate impressions of what lies behind the client's free associations. Since it is incumbent on the therapist every now and again to give interpretations that are as accurate as possible, he or she must discern the truth of what is taking place and this is not an easy matter because the client's statements can have a variety of possible meanings, as will now be shown.

Let us look at one statement that Jim made to his therapist. During a period of free association, he began to think that she had offered him no real help. Then in an anguished moment he said that she was in fact 'useless'.

First, this statement may reflect the truth of what had taken place so far. At least with this particular client and up to this point in time, the analyst might actually have been 'useless'. It is, of course, possible that if anyone looked closely at the so-called therapeutic process through which Jim had been passing, he or she might justifiably conclude that his analyst had not been helpful or – even worse – that Jim would have been better off if he had not commenced analysis.

Second, it may be that his complaint about her is a manifestation of transference. It is, in reality, a complaint about his father who offered Jim no real help with his problems. Jim now has the same expectations of his analyst. He takes the view that she also will not be able to help him.

The analyst may unwittingly provide a cue for this transference by behaving in ways that echo Jim's past. This sometimes happens because a client's behaviour encourages the therapist to adopt a certain social posture. Thus in the initial stages of therapy, Jim's analyst found herself becoming progressively more dominant. This was because Jim was behaving in the same submissive way in which he had behaved towards his father. He provided cues that created in the therapist the same feelings Jim's father had had. Hence she was 'set up' to behave like his father. If she *did* respond like his father, she would clearly trigger a whole set of reactions that Jim would have directed towards his father. It follows that, before offering an interpretation, she must check on the part she may be playing in the manifestation of transference and the contribution she has made to Jim's reactions.

Third, it may be that in reality Jim's problems are so deep-seated that they are highly resistant to change, so resistant that Jim's responses to therapy have so far been 'useless' ones. It could be said that it is not his therapist who is 'useless' but Jim. To admit this is too difficult for him, so he becomes involved in a process that Freud called projection (see Chapter 8) – what he could not accept in himself (that he was 'useless') he attributed to another person.

A fourth possibility is that Jim is frustrated and angry with his analyst, principally because her interpretations are beginning to make clear the extent of his psychological difficulties. The exposure of the problematic state he is in makes him feel frustrated. However, he fails to realise exactly why he is frustrated and blames the wrong thing – the analyst's performance. Paradoxically if she *were* ineffective (and therefore actually 'useless'), he would not be so angry.

A fifth possibility is that Jim wishes to know how much his analyst will tolerate before she treats him like his father did. Sensing a different kind of security than that which he had with his father, Jim is beginning to find out how far he can go without the analyst doing what his father did, suppressing his 'bad' behaviour by withdrawing from the relationship.

We have looked at five ways in which the client's statement can be interpreted. If now we turn to the analyst's reaction to the accusation that she is 'useless', we can imagine her making a number of statements to herself, each of which is open to being interpreted in as wide a range of ways as Jim's statement. For example, what she says to herself may be realistic or it may be a form of countertransference.

Attempting to arrive at the truth hidden beneath what is happening in analysis will involve a continual examination of what the client has said and its possible meanings and how she is personally reacting to this and why. Only a limited amount of this activity can be done in the therapy session itself, particularly if the analyst is lacking in experience. Nevertheless she will need to discern who is contributing what to the process of therapy (Casement, 1985).

In addition to being aware of the difficulties of interpreting any one statement, a therapist will bear in mind other considerations that will guide what is said to the client. In the first few sessions, he or she will not want to present the client with interpretations based on too little information. Comments will be made indicating simply that the client's utterances are being carefully considered.

The therapist will always offer an interpretation tentatively and will take note of how the client responds. A client may reject an interpretation because it is wrong but may also reject it because it is right. The therapist must discern which of these is most likely since rejection may be a form of resistance that has to be understood more fully. Where resistance occurs there may be persistent denial because this is the only course open to suppressing the intense and possibly chaotic emotions that recognition and acceptance of the truth might release. Usually the therapist will wish to avoid the rejection of an interpretation by choosing wisely the timing of its presentation.

Offering interpretations will be done with the hope of promoting further clarification and facilitating the generation of further thoughts and feelings. The therapist will not want to direct the client's thoughts or feelings or intrude into the process of the client's ongoing free associations.

Interpreting dreams

In addition to free association, the analysis of dreams is an aid to making further sense of unconscious processes. The client may be asked to describe any dreams he or she has had. This might take place at the beginning of a therapy session and might be followed by a request to freely associate to the images that appear in the dream so that the therapist can interpret them.

The nature of dream interpretation can be explained using the following example. (Incidentally, dreams are seldom as simple or as straightforward as suggested here.) A woman who was a union official reported a dream in which she had joined a night school class on philosophy. On her arrival at the class, she was surprised to find that the person teaching the class was a member of her union who was an office cleaner. Of course, since it would be highly unusual for an office cleaner to appear in the guise of a teacher of philosophy, this dream appears to be nonsense and may be dismissed as such.

We can, however, take each element of the dream and find out what it represents by using free association. For example, we could find out what a philosopher represents in the union official's experience. Let us suppose that we do this. We ask her to freely associate to the word 'philosopher' and find that the

only contact she had with a person calling himself a philosopher was at a party where, in response to his apparent arrogance and much to her satisfaction, he was taken down a peg
or two by someone who ridiculed some of his ideas. This picture
of what happened at the party gives us a clue as to what
'philosopher' represents or symbolises. It has come to represent
an arrogant person who should be taught a lesson.

It is this representation that the union official uses to 'clothe'
the office cleaner. We may suspect that for various reasons she
has an unconscious wish to see the office cleaner in a position
in which her arrogance (or what she takes to be her arrogance)
could be publicly ridiculed, and this is one possible meaning
that her dream is covertly expressing. Further free associations
to the dream's various parts would support or fail to support
this hypothesis, as would an examination of some of the union
official's more conscious attitudes.

We can see from this initial excursion into dream interpretation that the content of dreams can be divided into 'manifest'
and 'latent' contents. The former refers to the obvious or superficial meanings of events in the dream and is given in a simple
factual account. The latter refers to the hidden meanings
contained in the dream's images. These meanings are portrayed in a disguised form.

Freud regarded dreams as veiled expressions of unconscious
wishes. He also believed that certain images always have the
same meaning. A pointed object, for example, always represented the male penis and an enclosed space represented the
womb where, before birth, a person enjoyed a profound sense of
safety and security.

Dreams not only have manifest and latent contents but also
show evidence of 'condensation'. This means that a single
image in a dream may stand for a great many ideas. Thus Freud
pointed out that an interpretation of a dream may be five times
as long as the simple description of the dream itself. In the
above example, we could easily enlarge on what the symbol
'philosopher' represents – the typist disliked any man who

seemed cold and calculating (the philosopher ridiculed at the party was one such man), and the cleaner appeared to exhibit these tendencies.

What motivates the client's progress

Psychoanalysts believe that a person will seek a relationship in later life that enables him or her to come to terms with the problems of the parent–child relationship. This occurs even though these problems have never been recognised and may be so unconscious as to be out of reach of everyday awareness. As and when therapy allows, a person will recreate a past relationship and the kind of problems that went with it. Thus a problem that has been 'frozen' in the past can become 'unfrozen' through therapy (Winnicott, 1958).

In the kind of relationship that therapy makes possible, past problems begin to surface because there is, as it were, an unconscious drive to resolve or master them. In Jim's case there was an unconscious impulse to understand the difficulties inherent in his relationship with his father and an unrecognised intention to come to terms with the internal conflicts that had been created.

Casement (1985, p. 83) describes an interesting example of how a problem formed in the past can be relived and subsequently resolved in the present. Casement, who uses his study as a room for therapy, had been writing something that required him to consult several books. As a consequence he had left his desk in a state of disarray. On leaving a therapeutic session, one of his patients pointedly remarked on the rather messy state of his study. The effect of this was to create a dilemma, 'Do I tidy my desk and leave myself open to the accusation of having responded to his jibe, or do I let it remain as it is only to be criticised for the continuing mess on a future occasion?' This kind of dilemma for a therapist is often accompanied by a surprising amount of emotional disturbance, emotional disturbance which, as we shall see, has a significance determined by the patient's past.

Casement tried to figure out exactly what he wanted to do about the untidiness. He decided to clear away those books he no longer required and leave open on his desk those he wanted to continue consulting.

At the next session, the patient drew his attention to this 'pathetic' compromise; he accused Casement of doing neither one thing nor another. Casement explained why he had tidied only some of his books and went on to explore why at the end of the previous session comments had been made about the state of his desk. He discovered that these comments reproduced circumstances that regularly occurred in the relationship between the patient and his mother. In his youth his mother constantly criticised his behaviour, and even when he did what she had suggested she found fault with him. Perhaps not surprisingly it was particularly in the realm of untidiness that his mother was beyond pleasing. By casting himself in the role of his mother, the patient had reproduced almost exactly the kind of problem that was a regular feature of his early life.

The conclusion of psychoanalytic treatment

Sometimes a person, like Jim or Casement's patient, will try to use any close relationship to re-enact a problem from the past and so resolve it. When this happens the individual towards whom these activities are directed usually takes steps to put a stop to what is happening. Often this is because the person on the receiving end becomes the focus of some very powerful, transferential emotions.

The therapist, of course, adopts an opposite stance. Where conflicts are becoming clear, it is important that the therapist recognises and keeps in touch with whatever powerful emotions are being expressed. Not only does this enable their examination but it also demonstrates that they can be dealt with. If the therapist finds them unmanageable, the client's worst fears will be confirmed and he or she will end up in a more problematic state than before (Bion, 1967). It is therefore imperative that the therapist is able to survive whatever arises in therapy without collapsing or retaliating, since this is central to the client's recovery (Winnicott, 1971).

The style of relating to parents and the unresolved conflicts it has created are dealt with in psychoanalytic therapy essentially through their exposure. This is done by interpreting the client's responses. Psychoanalytic therapy concludes when problems of resistance and transference have been resolved. This may take some considerable time. The client is likely to be in therapy 1 hour a day, 5 days a week, for at least 6 months and maybe up to 3 years or longer.

6 SELF-ANALYSIS

SUMMARY

This chapter explains how the developing child is influenced by his or her early experiences in the family and how this influence can make itself felt in later life. Steps that can be taken to recognise connections between early and later experience are described. These steps are a necessary preliminary to the process of personal change, which is also described.

Introduction

The principles of self-analysis that are presented below are drawn from a number of writers. These include Karen Horney, particularly her book *Self-analysis* (Horney, 1942), Gottschalk (1989) and Southgate (1987). This chapter has been written not primarily to encourage the reader to engage in self-analysis but as a means of illustrating the link between past events belonging to a person's childhood and psychological problems that emerge in the present.

Learning how to get on with people in childhood

When infants are born into families, they have their first experience of human society. This experience will have lasting effects. One of the essential things that infants and children learn is how to make their way in the enclosed world of their family, and this will strongly influence how they will make their way with others outside the family. In other words children learn how to get on with or relate to others in ways that, in large measure, are determined by how they are treated and by the roles or positions assigned to them by their families.

Once a child has learned the patterns of behaviour that are used to relate to others, he or she uses them regularly, automatically and spontaneously. What we might describe as a 'method' of getting on with others developed at an early age becomes so habitual and so natural it can rarely be consciously examined. The question, 'Just how do you relate to others?' is a difficult one, and a person will normally answer that he or she 'just gets on with others' without being aware of how.

It is naturally quite possible for a child to be pushed into a role or way of relating that suits his or her family but does not suit the child; a child's outgoing, extrovert assertiveness can be cowed by a family that assigns the child a passive role more suited to the personality of an introvert. This tendency towards passivity can carry on into adult life. At this later time not only may it continue to be unrepresentative of a person's true personality but it may also give rise to passive forms of behaviour that are inappropriate for the situations in which it is expressed. In other words it is used inflexibly without discerning whether it is suitable or not.

In *Self-analysis* (1942) Karen Horney illustrates these problems and their consequences. She uses the example of Clare, a woman who conducted her own self-analysis after a period of therapy with a psychoanalyst.

Clare's personal history

Clare was essentially an unwanted child, the daughter of an attractive and dominant woman. Born after her brother, she was materially treated in a similar manner to him but she was not, as her brother was, the object of her mother's affection. Her brother received more admiration, concern and tenderness than she did and she found herself excluded from the mother–son relationship.

Clare's father, to whom she turned at one stage, was a devoted admirer of her mother. He showed no interest in his children and was unresponsive to any approaches that Clare made to him. Clare's mother despised him, and as a consequence the marriage was an unhappy one.

In response to her failure to achieve acceptance first with her mother and brother and then with her father, Clare felt insecure and something of a victim. Clare's mother and brother teased her about her tendency to appear a 'martyr', and their treatment of her led to the fixed conviction that she was unlikeable and that she was responsible for the way things were. Nevertheless she discovered a way out of her difficulties. She became one of her mother's admirers. Her mother now gave Clare the approval that dispelled her insecurity. At last she had found a place for herself in the world.

Imagine the effects of Clare's early experience on her personality and the way she learned to relate to others. She was born into a family where the only and most significant attachment was between her brother and her mother. From this she was excluded and some of her reactions to this exclusion were repudiated by her mother and her brother. These experiences formed her first taste of human society. They taught her that the successful way for her to get on with people and to be accepted by them was to admire them. This became a fixed conviction with her, an unquestioned assumption that formed the basis of her social behaviour. She related to her family by admiring them, and in later life she sought acceptance from others by admiring them too.

Clare's convictions about human relationships, which developed from her experiences in her family, gave her a deep-seated, spurious view of how to relate to others. She was committed to what could be described as a false 'theory' about how human relationships work, a 'theory' she manifested in her behaviour but was not aware of because it had become too natural a way of expressing herself.

Problems addressed by self-analysis

Self-analysis is concerned with linking problematic features of personal history, such as those exemplified in Clare, with current psychological problems or symptoms which that history generates. These symptoms can appear to be far removed from the true nature of their causes in the past and often appear to be inexplicable. For example, Clare complained of such things as a distrust of human relationships, of a lack of self-confidence, of being unaccountably inhibited when trying to fulfil some of her personal ambitions and of emotional fatigue affecting her work. These problems had a far from obvious link with her previous early life.

We can at this stage offer some speculations about Clare's psychological problems. Let us look at her distrust of social relationships and her lack of self-confidence. Clare had certain unspoken convictions about how relationships work, what has been described as her 'theory' of relationships – admiring people is the key to being accepted by them. When stated explicitly this is a very superficial view of human relationships and of what they have to offer. It implies that I am not accepted 'for myself' or for the unique qualities for which I should be valued but only for the admiration I supply. It also implies, as was the case with Clare, 'If people admire me I cannot accept this admiration as genuine. They do not really admire me. What they want from me is acceptance'.

Clare was not aware of the logic underlying her approach to relationships. What she *was* aware of were the consequences of this logic – a deep distrust of relationships and a lack of confidence in herself. Paradoxically although she felt her security lay in admiring others and possibly being admired by them, this actually left her relationships without genuine satisfaction.

Let us look at another of Clare's problems, which may again initially seem to be unconnected to her personal history. This problem concerns her failure to fulfil her ambitions. Clare was a journalist and found that she could not complete a book she was writing. She had made several attempts at this but always, inexplicably, failed. One possible reason for this is that in completing her book she would not be pleasing those close to her, such as her boyfriend. (He may have given her hints that he would not be happy – and it was Clare's role in life to please him and others – if she had a success that rivalled his own achievements. The view he took of this matter, incidentally, may have arisen from problems in the way *his* family treated *him* in his early years.)

The customary response to the symptoms that Clare complained about, her distrust of relationships, her lack of self-confidence and so on, is to seek some ready explanation for them, an explanation that prevents the search for a more fundamental understanding. Dissatisfaction with superficial explanations is an important incentive for engaging in self-analysis.

Analysing Clare's problems

The nature of Clare's problems became manifest first with the help of a psychoanalyst and then through her own work in self-analysis. Many of the discoveries she made about herself developed from an examination of her relationships, particularly her current relationship with her boyfriend. Essentially what she discovered was her compulsive modesty, her compulsive dependence on her partner and her compulsive need to appear superior to other people. Let us first examine what is meant by the word 'compulsive'. Then following this we will look at why such apparently incompatible processes as compulsive modesty and compulsive superiority can co-exist.

Turning first to the word 'compulsive', as we have seen, a person's life experience and fundamental assumptions about the nature of social relationships lead him or her to think and act in certain ways. Clare's experience in the family taught her that admiration of her mother was the key to being accepted. Thus Clare learned that acceptance by another person depended on her taking up a modest position. Early experience coerced her into involuntarily and frequently adopting this position in virtually all social relationships. She learned to do it so automatically that she was unaware of the way in which she behaved. Had she had some awareness, she might have thought that she *wished* to adopt this position. Actually she was driven 'compulsively' to do so by processes laid down in her personality in childhood. This resulted in her always adopting a modest and reticent social role whenever she met somebody new.

One of the important reasons for being compulsively modest was that, while she behaved modestly, she felt secure. The first time she gained this sense of security was in her family. Later she experienced it when she behaved modestly towards others. As we have seen this security was based on a false theory and was in itself ultimately unsatisfactory.

As well as the word 'compulsive' requiring some explanation, so does the co-existence of logically incompatible tendencies. Clare had *both* a compulsive modesty and a compulsive need to appear superior to others. Such incompatibility is possible since a person's early experience may result in the assumption that the more modest a person, the more superior he or she is. This is the logic of 'You will appreciate my superiority when you recognise how modest I am.'

Neurotic trends and how they are pursued indiscriminately

Clare's compulsive tendencies formed what Horney described as neurotic trends. A neurotic trend consists of forces in the personality of which a person is unaware and which are expressed in the form of unconscious striving. This striving is a response to such things as feelings of isolation and helplessness. In Clare's case we see how her isolation arose from being a child who was unwanted by her family. As we have shown acting out a neurotic trend in the form of a compulsive tendency brings a certain sense of security.

Because it is difficult to discern its operation, a neurotic trend can be expressed not only without a person's realisation but also too frequently and without a person taking into account its consequences. In other words it is expressed indiscriminately. Clare's compulsive dependence on her boyfriend provides a good example. While solving her fear of isolation, it drove her to disproportionate lengths to maintain a relationship with him. She could not see, as an outsider easily could, that he did not care about their relationship and that, while it continued, he took her for granted and treated her badly. Because of the strength of her wish for security, she could not fathom the true nature of what was taking place. She could neither express her dependence appropriately, tailoring it realistically to her circumstances, nor discern its consequences – that her boyfriend exploited the situation.

How to engage in self-analysis

Horney advocated the use of self-analysis because she thought that a person's motives to gain some insight into deep-seated, problematic, psychological processes can be strong enough to overcome the obstacles preventing their discovery and change. Many psychoanalysts would disagree with this since they believe that a person cannot deal with what is troubling him or her without specialist help.

Horney suggested using the same method for self-analysis as is used in psychoanalysis, namely free association. Free association involves complete and frank expression of feelings and allows a pattern of thought to develop without guidance or direction. A person lets thoughts come to mind without inhibition, no matter how odd or unusual they appear to be. Without reflecting on them such thoughts are noted down for later interpretation and analysis. What follows is an example of free association and how it can be used to make sense of experience.

Frank, a psychologist, knowing how psychoanalysts make use of free association, decided to use it to make sense of an experience that he had had in his early twenties. Frank completed his degree in psychology during a period of full employment but for the first 6 months after graduation he was unable to find a job. He described this period as one in which each day he was gripped by a mixture of dread and panic. The intensity of these feelings became progressively worse so that eventually he was living on the border of a mental breakdown.

Looking back on this time, although he appreciated that being without a job was unpleasant, he did not understand why his reaction to unemployment was so excessive and had such an unnerving effect on his mental health. He therefore began to freely associate to anything he could remember of this period. For example, he asked himself what came to mind when he thought of the word 'job'. A number of things occurred to him and one of these he saw as potentially significant.

Frank recalled an incident at school when he was 14 or 15. His English teacher complained to him that all the bright boys in the school did science. (Frank had been equally successful at all the subjects he took. He was as good at the arts, particularly English, as he was at the sciences.) Frank's teacher went on to beg him to consider developing the obvious talents he had for English. He remembered not answering her but inwardly he rejected her request. As far as he was concerned, it was in the sciences – and this was something he regarded as self-evident – that his own lucrative future lay. He would get a degree in a science subject and, when he had done this, the world, which would be in need of his services, would be there to reward him. This he assumed was inevitable.

Frank's view of his future, particularly his convictions and attitudes towards it, had been unself-consciously picked up from his parents, who, in a whole range of ways, again and again reinforced what initially he thought but later simply assumed. Their acceptance and approval of him was caught up with what he and they regarded as lying ahead him. This meant that something such as unemployment did not figure in what he took to be the realities of his future. If he had thought about it (which he hadn't), he would have had to admit that unemployment was *theoretically* possible. However, even this admission would have remained more theoretical than real.

Since some 10 years elapsed between the incident at school and his unemployment, we may suppose that the ideas he had about his future and the emotional certainty that went with them (that the world needed him, would reward him and everyone would approve of him) became an even more fixed conviction, a conviction around which much of his thinking had been organised. No doubt this conviction was so deep-seated that he was no longer aware of how much his views were based on it and how much emotional security he gained from it.

By freely associating to the word 'job', Frank discovered a memory that 'spoke volumes' about his past and its relationship to his severe bouts of anxiety. He unearthed some of the significant assumptions on which his life had been based. In not being able to gain employment, reality was contradicting what in his mind had been taken as real, such as an easily obtained, well-rewarded place in society. Had he fully understood this at the time of his near mental breakdown and been aware of the role his parents played, he could have adjusted better to a difficult situation, and, correcting his assumptions, his feelings of dread and panic would have subsided.

Dream analysis

The process of self-analysis can be helped by recording dreams and analysing them. Analysing a dream starts with freely associating to its different parts. Horney suggested that a dream is often a response to everyday circumstances that expresses specific tendencies in the personality. It is important therefore to link what provokes a dream with the tendencies it expresses.

We can easily use the example of Frank to illustrate the nature of dream analysis. Suppose that, instead of Frank recalling an actual incident like the one he had with his English teacher, he dreamt that he was back at school and his English teacher was trying to persuade him to do arts subjects such as English rather than science. If Frank freely associated to any aspects of the dream – freely associating to words like 'English', 'science' and 'the future' – he would be able to interpret this dream and draw the same conclusions from it as he had when he examined the actual incident.

Interpreting free associations and dreams

Once a written record of free associations has been made, this must be interpreted. The aim of interpretation is to get at the hidden meaning of feelings, thoughts, events and relationships in the past and the present. To make sense of hidden meanings, a person must use both intuition and reason, passing from one to the other. This involves, in Horney's view, first abstaining from reasoning and then 'not excluding it', sensing the connections between one thing and another and then turning to more deliberate reflection.

In exploring notes produced by free association, a person should be guided by curiosity and interest. Interpretations should be held tentatively and a person should not accept more than he or she can believe. The insights gained in this process can only be accepted one at a time, and each discovery or insight must be reworked in the light of further discoveries and insights.

Hindrances to progress

For the self-analyst progress will inevitably be hindered by the difficulty of examining emotionally significant areas of experience. This is known as resistance. In the process of going over notes, he or she will find issues that are avoided and mental digressions that lead away from more vital concerns. Resistances show themselves in specific forms such as self-protective emotional reactions and an inability to think clearly. These resistances can in themselves be examined by freely associating to their apparent causes.

Resistances arise because a pattern of neurotic trends gives a person security and, as a rule, a person's psychological processes protect him or her by making sure that any form of thought, feeling or behaviour that promotes security is not threatened. However, as we have seen in the case of Clare, the cost of defending security is psychological problems.

Progress may be hampered not only by resistances. The way forward may be blocked by an analysis that indicates that everything appears to be bad or everything appears to be good; or it may be blocked by a loss of incentive that could happen by too great an adherence to 'compulsively' regular periods of self-analysis. Nevertheless, with the right kind of persistence, resistances can be overcome.

Progress in self-analysis

There are three essential stages that chart progress in self-analysis. The first is the discovery of a neurotic trend. Such a discovery is encouraging and brings a sense of release because a person no longer feels the victim of incomprehensible and unidentifiable psychological forces.

The value of discovery should not be overestimated, however, since much of what the neurotic trend means may still lie hidden. Also a person may be willing to recognise and face up to a neurotic trend and may wish to understand it, but the desire to be honest is not the capacity to be honest. It is this capacity which must be developed. Therefore, encouraging as discovery is, it forms only the basis for further work.

A second stage involves identifying the hidden causes, manifestations and consequences of the neurotic trend. The neurotic trend will be found to be associated with a specific self-image, a specific view of what others are like and a particular kind of vulnerability. If we illustrate this from what we know of Clare, her compulsive modesty was associated with a humble self-image, with the view that other people always (and neverendingly) wished to be pleased and with the vulnerability caused by being taken for granted and being exploited. At this second stage an individual realises more fully the undesirable outcomes of the ways in which he or she automatically thinks and behaves and the limits set on spontaneity and personal development.

Discerning how a neurotic trend is working or functioning does not guarantee a cure for the problems it poses. However, like its discovery, gaining an understanding of what might be described as the 'dynamics' of the neurotic trend encourages further exploratory searching. While a deeper understanding is developing, a person will become more confident in looking at the false beliefs about the self and the more vulnerable aspects of personality. A distinction is increasingly drawn between how one ought to feel and how one actually feels. A person will also find that a more friendly attitude is developing towards him or herself and towards others.

In the third and final stage of self-analysis, the way in which the neurotic trend is related to other parts of the personality becomes clear. Of particular interest here is the way one neurotic trend lends support to others. This support becomes apparent whether a trend is compatible with others, a compulsive need for power existing alongside a compulsive need for prestige, or incompatible with others, as occurred with Clare – compulsive modesty co-existing with a compulsive need to appear superior to other people.

In the final stage of self-analysis, then, change in the personality is brought about by developing an understanding of how one feature of personality relates to other features. For this reason a person should not be content with isolated solutions to his or her problems since these solutions do not take into account relations between different aspects of the personality.

An illustration of the three stages of self-analysis

In order to illustrate the three stages of self-analysis, if only briefly and superficially, consider the following example. This is a fragment of a man's self-analysis.

Having read some of the literature on self-analysis, a businessman, Lawrence, who regarded himself as (wholly) logical and rational began to examine whether there was anything in his thoughts or behaviour that needed explaining. Cursory reflections yielded nothing and he was tempted to conclude, 'No, everything I do is rational and logical and does not require explanation.' He decided, however, to override this initial conviction and persist. He then discovered a piece of his own behaviour for which there was no logical explanation.

Commuting home by train he always had to change trains a few stops before his home station. The train he changed to was going to one of two destinations, Chester or Helsby. However, the train bound for either destination always stopped at his home station. Occasionally as he changed trains he would be approached by a person asking him whether the next train was bound for Chester or Helsby. Although he usually knew the answer to this question, he always directed the person to someone else, explaining that he was going only a few stops down the line and implying, although this was not true, that he did not know the final destination of the train. Why if he knew where the train was going did he not divulge this information? Although it had not struck him before, this was clearly an irrational piece of behaviour that needed explaining.

Freely associating to the image of this situation of a person asking him the train's destination, the most promising suggestion (of several) that came to mind was that, when a situation occurred in which he had a choice about taking or refusing to take any responsibility for another person's actions, he (compulsively) chose not to. This is the first stage of self-analysis, the discovery of a neurotic trend.

The second stage is the discovery of the causes, manifestations and consequences of this tendency. Looking at other areas of his life, this businessman discovered other forms of his desire to avoid responsibility. In supervising his junior staff, for example, he now realised that he went to inordinate lengths to make sure his advice was clear to them, writing down for them everything he had said. Although he flattered himself about his efficiency, the real motive behind this was to make them wholly responsible for their actions. If at any time his junior staff were criticised by his boss, he could deny responsibility by pointing to the thoroughness of his supervision and finding the appropriate written memorandum, copies of which he scrupulously retained.

Lawrence also found a link between his attitudes to money and his choosing not to take responsibility for others. Although not irresponsible, he had no sense of financial responsibility towards his family. This had always been something that puzzled him since many of his colleagues took their financial responsibilities towards their wives and children very seriously and, unlike him, had done such things as arrange life and mortgage insurance. He knew that he differed from them in this but had no idea why.

Looking for possible causes of his hitherto unconscious attitudes to avoiding responsibility, he examined his parents' attitudes towards responsibility, attitudes he had been exposed to as a child. He was surprised to find how much his attitudes mimicked those of his father. In fact his surprise bordered on shock since he had always thought of himself as entirely different from his father.

There is much more that could be written about this second stage, but let us move on to the third. This man, in addition to compulsively choosing not to take responsibility for others, was also compulsively unselfish. In the family in which he had grown up, an acceptable place amongst them depended on him behaving in an unselfish manner. Linking these two aspects of his personality was a (too) democratic attitude towards people. He believed that people should (always) choose for themselves and be responsible for themselves. This would normally be regarded as praiseworthy, but he used his unselfishness and democratic outlook to avoid taking responsibility in situations where problems could be easily resolved by his leadership and expertise. In these situations he simply refused to become involved.

This lack of involvement was conspicuously demonstrated in his relationship with his children, in which excessively democratic attitudes and a refusal to take responsibility resulted in his children's wild and occasionally dangerous behaviour. His children's behaviour was tolerated or ignored but not constructively dealt with. He had never, until now, understood the criticisms his wife made of his attitudes towards his children.

An interesting feature of this analysis is the way it identifies a number of attributes that are usually highly valued, such as efficiency, unselfishness and a democratic outlook, and explains them in terms of compulsive tendencies. If we take unselfishness as an example, it is of course generally to be commended. Its place in Lawrence's personality was not, however, the consequence of a moral or ethical outlook. It was not a consciously thought out moral value to which he subscribed. Rather it arose from early experience in his family and was the price of gaining acceptance from others. His unselfishness now operates not for the sake of other people but for his sake. Paradoxically he is unselfish for selfish reasons.

Obviously it is easy for a person to defend a compulsive form of unselfishness on the grounds of it being a virtue. Similarly many other compulsive tendencies can be presented in a flattering light and rationalised as virtues – compulsive dependence can be interpreted as affection, compulsive modesty as humility and so on.

The feasibility of self-analysis

The feasibility of self-analysis is a debateable issue. A psychoanalyst who argues against self-analysis is likely to point out the advantages that a helpful relationship with a therapist offers. This relationship provides an opportunity for the client to re-enact some of the interpersonal problems that were part of the client's early history. The therapist can also see the issues that are involved more objectively.

In contrast to these arguments it can be said that self-analysis offers some advantages of its own. The self-analyst, being less reliant on a single relationship (between him or herself and the therapist) can become an observer of a wide range of interactions with others. This is also true when it comes to looking at personal, psychological processes to which he or she has easier access than that of the therapist.

There are types of people who will not benefit from self-analysis and are unlikely to engage in it. First, a person may have personality processes that are so mutually reinforcing that they form a structure that is strong enough to resist all attempt at change. Second, a person may have a very rewarding neurotic trend. A compulsive need to exercise power over others, for instance, may bring many rewards. Such an exercise of power may be more appealing than turning to more constructive ways of living. This will be particularly so if people submit to it and thereby collude with it.

What has just been described spells doom for any progress in analysis. However, these processes are unlikely to be the only ones active in the personality. In most people there are, in addition to destructive processes, those that are genuine and constructive. Authors who encourage others to take up self-analysis (Southgate, 1987; Gottschalk, 1989) take the view that it is unlikely that the drive towards resolving psychological problems will be so weak as to stop a person from pursuing their own analysis and deriving some benefits from it.

7 Psychoanalytic Approaches to Child Development

Summary

Two differing psychoanalytic views of child development will be examined in this chapter. The first is the one that was originally proposed by Freud.

The second, object relations theory, which is more recent, focuses on the influence of the very early months and years of a child's life. Some of the implications of this theory's description of early life for adult years are examined by looking at psychological differences between boys and girls.

Introduction

Freud thought that at each stage of development a child's attention was focused on different sensitive areas of his or her body. The child is preoccupied with first one area then another in a biologically determined sequence. This sequence is described in the first part of this chapter.

Freud did not make systematic observations of children. He relied exclusively on the information he gained from his adult patients for his theory of child development. Many who used Freud's theory in their work with children found it wanting. Amongst these people were a group of psychoanalysts who have come to be known as object relations theorists.

Unlike Freud, who believed that the years of childhood up to the age of 7 years were the most important in the formation of the personality, those of the object relations school see the first few months and years of life as having a crucial influence. In this period of life, thinking and language skills have not developed and the child cannot therefore describe his or her experiences. Explaining what is taking place at this time must therefore involve a certain amount of conjecture. Object relations theorists claim, however, that we can gain some access to the infant and child's psychological processes by observing and then interpreting their play.

Those who have done research on marital problems and mental health (Hafner, 1985) and who have worked in the area of women's therapy (Eichenbaum and Orbach, 1984) have found object relations theory a fruitful source of insight into psychological differences between male and female and their relationships with each other. These matters will be addressed in the latter part of this chapter.

Freud's view of personality development

According to Freud there are five stages of development. Each of these is dominated by an area of the body that is sensitive to stimulation, and this is referred to as an 'erogenous zone'. Using the term more broadly than is now customary, he regarded the pleasurable stimulation of an erogenous zone as creating 'sexual' sensations.

Individuality is determined by the way in which the child manages the journey through the five stages of development. These stages merge into each other rather than being clearly separated, and the prominence of each will vary in different children.

How a child negotiates each stage will be influenced by such factors as the way the parents deal with or treat the child, their attitudes towards him or her and the child's experience of pleasure, punishment and pain. Whatever experiences the child has, they will form the basis of the adult personality.

The oral stage

The term 'oral stage' is a label for the period in which the mouth or 'oral cavity' gives rise to experiences that have a dominant influence in the first 2 years of a child's life. In the oral stage, the child learns about and relates to the world through his or her mouth. This is partly because of the sensitivity of the mouth parts and partly because of the stimulation received during the feeding process, which is associated with the potent needs of hunger and thirst.

The mouth, then, is the dominant mode of learning about the world. Thus if the child is fed on demand, he or she experiences a need being met by a world that is on hand to satisfy that need; this may lead to the constant feeling that the world is a secure place and this in turn becomes the basis of the personality characteristic of optimism. Conversely, an infant's experience of being left hungry for long periods before being fed becomes the basis of pessimism.

This example illustrates how experience takes on or 'symbolises' certain meanings. The experience of needs being quickly met has come to mean or symbolise something else, that the world is a good place in which to be. This process of symbolisation is an important one since the infant is at a stage when language has not yet been properly acquired and the meaning of experience cannot be consciously thought out in words. This same process of symbolisation is an important feature of other experiences and other stages of development.

The oral stage is divided into two substages, the first of which, the oral incorporative, is dominated by the pleasures of sucking and taking in. Because of sensuous or 'sexual' feelings associated with the mouth and lips, satisfaction is gained from any kind of stimulation occurring in the absence of food. Also the pleasures of this stage can be reinstated in later life in such activities as chewing, kissing, drinking and smoking.

The second substage, the oral aggressive, is the stage of teething and weaning. The infant finds the mother a source of pleasure and frustration. In the case of the latter, assuming the mother is breastfeeding, frustration may occur because the infant is being weaned or because, as sometimes happens during teething, the infant has taken to biting his or her mother's nipple. The infant's positive and negative experiences will give rise to ambivalent feelings about the mother that form the basis of love and hate. Aggression expressed by biting the mother can take on more symbolic forms in later life – the mouth parts are again used to express aggression but in the form of 'biting' sarcasm.

Terms such as 'oral' that refer to important aspects of development can be used to describe certain types of people. Thus a psychoanalyst may describe as an 'oral character' a patient who relates to others in a way that implies 'Take care of me by feeding me and looking after me.' Such a person may well equate being loved with being entertained to good meals or being given gifts.

The anal stage

In this stage the focus of attention is drawn to the activities of toilet training, which have their characteristic rewards and punishments and engender certain kinds of relationships between children and their parents. The child must take responsibility for certain actions, principally the control of bowel movements, and must give up the pleasure of indiscriminate elimination. The praise of parents for successful bowel movements may lead the child to believe that he or she has presented the parents with a gift, and this may result in the creation of a generous personality. Alternatively, the pleasurable sensations a child may have in retaining his or her faeces may be reflected later in miserliness – 'What I have I keep.'

Important attitudes to cleanliness, neatness and tidiness are laid down in this stage, attitudes that may develop into tendencies to make fine distinctions or into intolerance of ambiguity. Freud regarded the anal personality as possessing three co-existing characteristics – orderliness, parsimony (that is a carefulness that borders on meanness) and obstinacy.

The anal stage is the first time that society, in the form of the child's parents, seeks to control a significant impulse, that of elimination. Being the child's first encounter with social control, the experiences of this stage may have far-reaching effects.

The phallic stage

This stage begins at that age of 3 or 4 and goes on until 6 or 7. It is a stage that is dominated, in the boy, by the Oedipus complex and, in the girl, by the Electra complex.

'Oedipus complex' is a term derived from a Greek tragedy in which the central figure, Oedipus, kills his father and marries his mother. In Freud's theory it involves the boy's desire for a close relationship with his mother, permeated with a strong though ill-defined sexuality, and, because of a sense of rivalry, a fear of his father. Possibly because of what he knows of the lack of an external genital organ in females, he fears that his jealous father will punish him by removing his genital organs. The boy resolves these fears by 'identifying' with his father, which means aligning himself with his father by unconsciously imitating him. By imitating and becoming more like him, he receives some of the rewards that are available to his father. The experiences of the phallic stage, however ill defined, are repressed because of their associated anxieties.

Freud was not as explicit in describing the phallic stage in female children. The term that has been used to described this phase in girls is the 'Electra complex'. For the girl, the Electra complex involves rivalry with the mother, desire for the father, the girl's belief that she has been castrated and the compensating discovery that she can have babies whereas men cannot.

The latency period

In the latency period no significant changes in personality occur. This is a sexually quiescent period. The child, however, continues to learn and acquire knowledge, skills and roles.

The genital stage

Throughout early development the child's preoccupation with sexual, biological processes makes him or her self-centred. With the reactivation of sexual impulses in puberty, the adolescent establishes relationships that are more outgoing and altruistic in nature. Choice of a partner towards which the adolescent moves will not, however, be independent of former experiences. In the case of the male, for example, the experiences of the phallic stage and the manner in which the Oedipus complex has been resolved may be particularly influential, the adolescent choosing, perhaps, a partner whose character is like that of his mother or whose character is the opposite of his mother's.

The object relations view of child development

In many ways the description of child development given by object relations theorists stands in sharp contrast to that of Freud (Klein and Tribich, 1981). They take the view that it is relationships rather than biology that are of primary importance.

According to object relations theory, during the first few months and years of life the infant's mind is made up of various images that represent reality. As these images are not necessarily accurate ones, they are referred to as 'objects'. 'Objects' symbolise people or aspects of people and always incorporate something of the relationship the infant has with these people. Children's play demonstrates the importance of objects. In play vast amounts of energy are expended constructing a world of people and the relationships between them.

Of all the relationships a child has, the one with the major caretaker, usually the mother, is of most importance. In their focus on the mother, object relations theorists differ from Freud, who regarded the father as more important. They believe that, since the mother is the most significant figure in the infant's life, her relationship with him or her provides the template for future relationships.

The infant relies on the mother for her caring love and attention and her ability to sense what he or she is feeling. When the infant is hungry, too hot or too cold, a sensitive mother becomes aware of this and takes steps to ameliorate the situation. While a particular need dominates the infant's mind, it may be associated with strong emotions that can feel unmanageable and overwhelming. However, the mother can make sense of what the child is experiencing and can convey her understanding of this by the actions she takes.

An important implication of this process of communication between mother and infant is that the infant can learn that apparently overwhelming feelings are in fact manageable. What is eventually internalised by the child is that another person can sense certain feelings and deal with them, and this can lead to the conviction that just as the mother has coped, he or she can also cope.

This process of empathic contact with a set of feelings, their acceptance and the demonstration that they are manageable is known as 'holding' or 'containment' (Winnicott, 1971). Holding or containment is important not only for children but also for adults undergoing therapy. In psychoanalysis, for example, in which a client may express strong and sometimes frightening emotions that up to the commencement of therapy had to be held in check, often by unconscious processes, the analyst must be in empathic contact with them and demonstrate that they are not indigestible.

The organisation of images

In the very earliest stages of life, the infant has not recognised the difference between him or herself and the outside world.

This means that what comes from where is altogether unclear in the accumulating mishmash of images. The infant does not make a distinction between what stems from self and what comes from the mother. In fact the merging or interpenetrating of the two means that the infant initially has a very poorly developed sense of self.

However, the accumulation of images is not without a form of organisation. Images are separated into 'good' and 'bad': those that are associated with the fulfilment of needs or the gratification of wishes, and those associated with unfulfilled needs or the frustration of wishes. The infant uses a method of categorising or organising images that is similar to one sometimes used in adult life. For example, suppose a person has lost an argument but continues to remain utterly convinced of the validity of his or her views. The events of the argument will be relived over and over again and its course imaginatively reconstructed. A person will dwell on what could and should have been said and, at least in imagination, may produce a more satisfactory, perhaps even victoriously triumphant, outcome. By thinking of what might have been said, this person will manipulate the images in the same as an infant does. Play is another example of this manipulative process since it often demonstrates the child's need to examine and control, through the use of imagination, the feelings that arise from transactions with people.

The process by which good images are separated from bad is known as 'splitting'. Hence good aspects of the mother are kept separate from and uncontaminated by what is experienced as bad. Of course, since no mother can provide only good experiences even under the best of circumstances, a child will know the world as split. Although good experiences hopefully outweigh bad, there are bound to be times when the infant feels hungry or cold and is denied physical contact. Massie (1982) incidentally suggests that bad experiences, provided they are of an everyday, nontraumatic kind, may well be necessary for psychological growth, although it is important that they occur in the context of a generally positive relationship.

Another aspect of the organisation of images concerns the way those occurring at an early stage do not just disappear but are overlaid by later ones. Earlier images exist at deeper, unconscious levels in the personality. They are also simpler or more primitive as they belong to a stage preceding the development of thinking and language skills that make possible the conscious, rational examination of experience. An example of the split between good and bad operating in a simple way is the tendency to divide people into good and bad, idealising the former and vilifying the latter. This tendency can have serious and far-reaching consequences. Idealisation, for instance, sometimes plays a significant part in marital choice, as can be seen from the following example.

Imagine a girl who has grown up in deprived circumstances, receiving from her socially unresponsive parents little by way of care and attention. In infancy and early childhood, the few good images her experience afforded her were grouped together. The rare occasions on which her parents or other people behaved positively towards her gave her a taste for the kind of relationship that would satisfy all her needs. Her good experiences have made it possible for her to imagine such a relationship with an ideal or idealised person.

Let us suppose that she imagines this person to be her marriage partner. In her projected future she now sees a haven of bliss in which she is treasured and understood and in which she receives gratification of the needs that her parents left largely unsatisfied. Eventually she meets someone who she sees as a potential marriage partner and she seizes the opportunity to escape from her family. As Dicks (1967) has pointed out, the more emotionally deprived the background from which she comes, the more intense her needs and the greater is her tendency to idealise her future husband. Needless to say the marriage relationship cannot live up to her expectations. The greater her idealisation, the greater her sense of disillusion when her partner fails to match up to what is expected of him.

Sometimes the process of idealisation is counterbalanced by that of vilification. A man who has entered the intimate relationship of marriage may have influential, early images of a good mother co-existing with images of a bad mother. When his wife satisfies his needs, he idealises her but when she fails to satisfy his needs, he believes she is the worst woman he has ever known and treats her accordingly.

Unrealistic, idealised, positive expectations may sometimes apply not to the marriage partner but to the marriage relationship itself. Partners may insist on there 'never being a cross word between them'. This is a mutual attempt to force each other to conform to an ideal. Consequently they must restrain, deny or unhealthily 'bottle up' the inevitable and natural frustrations that arise when two people live together.

When an idealised image of the partner or the marriage relationship is maintained, it is usually done in a compulsive manner. The partners are psychologically coerced or unconsciously driven by their very early history to think and act in certain ways. As a consequence the marriage may become routine, conventional, relatively lifeless and even futile, with the partners unable to engage each other on the basis of genuine feelings in a meaningful and mutually satisfying way.

Stages in development

At the beginning of the infant's life, images represent parts of people or objects. Later they come to represent whole persons, and finally they contribute to the development of a sense of self. With regard to part objects, Melanie Klein (1952) has written of the 'good breast' and the 'bad breast', each symbolising different experiences in the process of infant feeding. Eventually the infant moves from taking in aspects of objects to the recognition and internalisation of objects as a whole. Stable representations of the mother may occur as early as 5 or 6 months of age, although their consolidation may take a year or two to complete. Since it involves the recognition of a person separate from the self, this consolidation is an important stage in offsetting the process of splitting.

An image of the mother as a whole object promotes the child's security since it can be used to represent her presence when she is no longer in sight. This then reduces the frightening sense of abandonment an infant may have whenever, however briefly, the mother is absent. With the development of language the child can converse not only with the external mother but also with the image of the mother within. Again this activity is often seen in play, either explicitly or in a symbolised form.

Not only does recognition of a separate person counteract some of the effects of splitting but it also encourages the coming together of the elements that form identity and a sense of self. The child can then envisage him or herself taking up a specific role and can come to have some understanding of how another person can complement this role.

The self is a complex configuration of multiple object relations that make up a person's inner sense of who he or she is. We become who we are by working on the objects that have been internalised and transforming them into a sense of self. Whether the self is experienced as good or bad is determined by early relationships. The mother plays an important role in this since her different aspects inhabit the inner world of the child. A child feels desirable and loved when the mother has provided experiences that give rise to good internal objects. Bad experiences lead to the child feeling unloved and unwanted. Sometimes because of the pain associated with these experiences, the child may lose all conscious access to them; that is, they become unconscious.

There are other aspects of the child's relationship with the mother that are internalised and become part of the self. For example, the degree to which a child has been dependent on the mother becomes the degree to which the child (and later the adult) expects him or herself to be dependent. What a dependent child comes to learn is that to be good (that is to be loved, accepted and valued) is to be weak and helpless. This becomes a feature of the inner self object representation and an integral part of the self. Once it is part of the experience of self, it forms the basis of external relations with others. Dependent individuals seek out relationships in which 'helplessness' is a dominant theme and the desire to find and create such relationships takes on a driven character. Once inner object relations are incorporated into the self like this, an individual may have little choice in following their dictates.

Not only are experiences in the mother–child relationship related to the child's sense of self but so also is the manipulation of images. A child who has a poor relationship with his or her parents has a choice of whether to believe that self is bad or that the parents are bad. There are certain advantages in seeing self as bad; the child can gain some comfort from imagining that he or she can behave in ways that obtain from the parents the love and support that is needed, and this is preferable to the catastrophic conclusion that the parents are unreliable, uncaring and prepared psychologically to abandon the child. Thus seeing the self as bad results in security, although at the cost of low self-esteem.

Unconscious imitation

The period in which the mother is seen as a separate human being sets the stage for the development of a sense of self. This is because it is possible for a child to suppose that the mother is in some respects like self and can then discern those elements of the mother's personality and behaviour that can be incorporated into his or her personality. This process of incorporation takes place through what is termed 'identification'. In identification the infant or child unconsciously takes on an observed characteristic by internalising it and imitating it. For example, the infant and child sees the mother behaving affectionately. What is seen is taken in and then used as the basis for imitating the mother's affectionate behaviour.

Illustrating the importance and nature of identification for personality development, Storr (1963) has described the following steps that a child may take. Within the child's personality, there are a number of potential personality traits that need to be developed, such as the capacity for becoming affectionate. He or she then observes an individual in whom these potential characteristics have been made actual. By copying this individual the child in turn begins to make actual his or her potential.

In line with object relations theory, identification is another process by which something outside the child is taken in or internalised. In this case it is an internalisation of a personality characteristic deriving from a person taken to be like oneself.

The fact that the earliest figure with whom both boys and girls identify is the mother has far-reaching consequences for the development of both sexes and for the kind of intimacy that they can enjoy with each other. In describing these processes it is important to recognise that we are not necessarily examining actual events. Rather we are looking at the kinds of image or object that are generated in a child's mind and the consequences that follow.

The male child's development

In the early years the mother satisfies a number of fundamental needs for her male child. She is sensitive to his need for food and drink and for physical comfort, and picks up the signals about his general emotional state. Given this sensitivity she provides the kind of person on whom he can depend. She is also a model through whom the child can develop certain of his personality characteristics. These characteristics are bound to include those necessary for caring for another person and forming attachments – characteristics such as affection and sensitivity to the emotional needs of others.

However, there comes a point in the male child's development when he realises that there is a significant difference between himself and his mother – to state the obvious, that he is male and she is female. Appropriate models for the child, therefore, are male, and it is identifying with these models that will lead to the internalisation of a set of qualities entirely different from those gained from his mother. In our culture such qualities include independence, strength and emotional control.

The male child's realisation that he must incorporate and develop the characteristics of males is one that his mother is likely to encourage by at least to some degree detaching herself from him so that he can develop his male autonomy. He will find himself, in the words of Lillian Rubin (1985, p. 57) 'abandoned to the shadowy world of men'.

He is unlikely to gain from his father what he lost from his mother. In turning to his father the child will not be internalising a person whose primary role is caring but a person who models self-containment. The father does not customarily demonstrate those features of personality necessary for attachment.

In turning to his father he must renounce his connection to the first person he identified with, his mother, and must now suppress certain female characteristics that have started to become a part of him so that he can bring his maleness to the fore. He may now fear the expression of any emotions other than those ordinarily permitted in the male – assertion (or its stronger form aggression) being one of the few. The achievement of his maleness is constantly threatened by the female that has developed within and which he may learn to fear and denigrate. Such fear and denigration is easily transformed into a distrust and prejudice against all things feminine, including, of course, women.

There may be another potent reason for despising women and being angry and frustrated with them. He may have experienced his mother as the person who broke his first attachment and deserted him. His resentment about this, which may well be deep-seated, unconscious and carried in the primitive images of early childhood, may manifest itself not just in the denigration of women generally but also in the fear of intimacy. Entering an intimate relationship with another woman is a reminder of the kind of relationship he had with his mother before it ended in abandonment.

It will not just be with women that these problems of intimacy and attachment make themselves felt. If we look at male friendships, they tend generally to be shallow and superficial. In fact most men have few or no socially intimate relationships with other men in which trust is sufficiently strong to invite self-disclosure (self-disclosure being a necessary ingredient of intimacy). Social interaction between most men is based on interests such as sport and work, rather than matters of a psychologically significant nature. If a man *does* have a socially intimate relationship, it is likely to be with a woman, which may reflect the strength of the earlier attachment to his mother and the strength of his distrust of other men.

The poor state of men's relationships with each other reflects a number of other factors. For example, many men follow the self-contained model of their fathers and therefore have neither the inclination nor, perhaps, the capacity for intimacy. Second, most men do not realise that they have the same feelings of vulnerability, fear and dependency as other men. They assume that other men are 'real' men and believe that if they disclosed some of their feelings other men would question their virility and despise them.

Of course, not all fathers will offer a wholly autonomous model. If a boy's father manages in his own personality to accept and integrate the psychological processes necessary for attachment and other characteristics that are regarded as feminine, he will then offer his son a well-adjusted model. If, however, in his own early life, he experienced an abandonment by his mother and a father who was psychologically distant and detached he is unlikely to offer his son much help.

Insofar as a boy's father models only such things as independence and self-containment, the boy will be encouraged to strengthen the boundaries of his own personality. This encouragement may be needed since if, at an earlier stage, he modelled himself on the empathic capacities of his mother, the distress of another person may easily make contact with his inner life and create emotions that he feels he may not be able to handle and which threaten his masculine, emotionally controlled self. If he does not guard the boundaries of his personality, he will, from time to time, feel invaded by the emotional states of others. However, making himself impermeable to the emotions of others will affect his capacity for intimacy, especially with anyone who wishes to be close to him.

The female child's development

Like a son a daughter early in life identifies with her mother and develops her mother's characteristics. Unlike a son there is no break in this process. As a result a girl experiences herself as more like her mother, perhaps eventually finding she has difficulty discovering where she ends and where her mother begins. This makes the development of autonomy difficult and the bond between mother and daughter may never be completely severed.

In a girl, female characteristics such as affection, emotional expressivity and sensitivity to the needs of others can fully develop since the mother continues to model the female role within the family. Demonstrating the nature of attachment, her role is one of primary caregiver who looks after the physical needs of her family and is sensitive to whatever emotional state they are in. A mother may often put the needs of others above her own.

Thus her daughter develops her capacity for attachment and her understanding of the emotional needs of others. As a consequence she has no difficulty attaching herself to another, perhaps with an ease and openness that is problematic (Eichenbaum and Orbach, 1984). Not only this but also her understanding of the emotions of others leads her into a natural empathic involvement. She participates in their emotional states. This contrasts starkly with the position of the male who is likely to end up with a weakened capacity for attachment. Also contrasting with the male is the attractiveness of friendships for the female because these will generally be experienced as satisfying the need for intimacy without the fear of being emotionally invaded.

It is important to understand the situation the mother is in since this will affect the way she relates to her daughter, which will in turn affect the characteristics that will be internalised. If her husband is strong, independent and expresses only a very limited range of emotions, he is unlikely to have met her needs. His efforts at self-containment and the maintenance of psychological distance will make him a person in whom she cannot confide and on whom she cannot depend.

Since she regards her self-esteem as resting on the success of her role as one who gives to others, she may not be aware of how some of her aims to meet the needs of others have taken precedence over certain of her own unfulfilled needs. She may simply experience a general sense of dissatisfaction. In spite of this she may well communicate to her daughter that ultimately her daughter will form a long-term relationship with a man on whom she can depend and who will satisfy her needs.

There are several consequences for the mother–daughter relationship as a result of this state of affairs. The mother may bring her own unmet needs to her relationship with her daughter. Alternatively she may react to her daughter's needs as if they were her own, reacting with dislike and perhaps denying them in herself and for her daughter. A third possibility is that her feelings about her own needs may be confused and unclear, and as a result she treats her daughter, who reminds her of deeply buried needs, with great ambivalence, sometimes gratifying her daughter's needs but at other times being more distant and hostile.

It is not only the girl's contact with her mother that is important but also her contact with her father. As with boys a father who integrates what are commonly regarded as masculine and feminine characteristics will offer a good model to his daughter. She will be able to integrate in herself natural tendencies towards autonomy and independence with characteristics that make attachments possible.

8 FREUD'S THEORY OF PERSONALITY

SUMMARY

This chapter describes the nature of personality and the way in which it functions. According to Freud mental processes occur on a number of levels, the unconscious being the most important of these. Also mental processes can be divided into three different types: biological, rational and moral.

In order to illustrate how the personality (as Freud envisaged it) works, a set of processes known as defence mechanisms will be described. A consideration of these will demonstrate how types of psychological function operate on different levels.

Introduction

In 1939, the year of his death, Freud wrote a final version of his theory of personality (Freud, 1949). In order to illustrate how he saw the various parts of the personality working, we will look at the way the rational processes in the personality defend themselves against the more irrational. This is done by means of defence mechanisms. Knowledge of these mechanisms has been further extended since Freud discovered them (A. Freud, 1936; Conte and Plutchik, 1995).

Three levels of mental functioning

Freud recognised three levels of mental functioning: the conscious, the preconscious and the unconscious. The conscious refers to current ongoing awareness. Although it is difficult to define the nature of consciousness precisely, we can say a number of things about it. Consciousness can be regarded as the middle ground between what is going on inside and what is going on outside a person. It is on this ground that what is inside is related to what is outside.

As you read these words that occupy 'current ongoing awareness', you are (hopefully) relating the desire to know about psychoanalysis (something inside you) with the ideas presented here (something outside you). If you already have a view about psychoanalysis, you will be comparing this view (something inside) with what I am currently suggesting (something outside).

The preconscious, the second level of mental functioning identified by Freud, refers to things going on in the mind that are readily accessible to awareness and that can consequently be made conscious at will. The preconscious contains memories and forms of stimulation that a person can make him or herself aware of. A reader of this text, for example, perhaps caught up in a process of encroaching boredom, may let his or her mind wander away from what is presented here and may resurrect more interesting material from the preconscious, memories of a recent night out or a holiday perhaps. Alternatively, encroaching boredom may make the reader aware of the effect of a chair on an increasingly numb rear end!

The third level of mental functioning, the unconscious, refers to what cannot be made conscious at will. In Freud's view unconscious processes, those of which a person is totally unaware, constitute the largest and most significant part of personality functioning. He had a keen interest in these and saw them as the most significant motivating forces in the personality. For example, if you were asked why you are reading this text, no doubt rational reasons (the preconscious being made conscious) are likely to come to mind. However, there are important psychological processes taking place outside your awareness, in your unconscious, and these have led you, or more accurately *driven* you, to examine this text.

Pulver (cited in Caputi, 1984) has made a useful distinction between what he termed the 'descriptive' and the 'dynamic' unconscious. The descriptive unconscious contains the thoughts and feelings that have been experienced but can no longer be recalled – this is where most of the ideas you read here and the thoughts and feelings you have about them will be in a week's time. The dynamic unconscious is more like a psychological world to which a person does not have access, which is made up of instincts, impulses, wishes, fears and so on that act and react on each other and in a clandestine way influence everyday life. It was the activity of the dynamic unconscious that was of major concern to Freud (Menaker, 1991).

Three types of process

In addition to identifying three levels of mental functioning, Freud also recognised three types of processes in the personality. These he referred to as id, ego and superego. Each of these terms is a label to cover a set of psychological functions that Freud grouped together.

Id is the latin word for 'it' and points to a set of biological processes that operate impersonally. The activities of the id form the foundation of the personality and represent the animal and impulsive side of a person's nature.

The id is made up of two types of instinct, the life instincts – hunger, thirst and sex – which act to create and maintain life, and the death instincts, which are aggressive and destructive. The life instincts operate using a form of energy known as libido.

When a baby comes into the world, his or her personality is made up wholly of id. At this stage psychological processes are dominated by the biological. The baby eats, sleeps and eliminates. As time goes by the ego, the Latin word meaning 'I' or 'me', develops from the id. The ego is a label for the rational part of the personality that includes perceiving, thinking and remembering.

Ego processes deal with the external world in a way which gains for a person what he or she needs. Thus they are important elements of conscious functioning and, in line with the explanation of consciousness given above, they connect what is inside a person, particularly needs, with what is outside, the environment where needs can be satisfied.

Although the id's needs, such as hunger and thirst, achieve some representation in the ego, the id itself operates at a wholly unconscious level. Since it is a part of the personality that does not include rational processes – these are present only in the ego – the id exists in a somewhat unusual state, one which is difficult to describe. However, this state is in one important respect like a dream. In a dream a person suspends some of the rationality that dominates waking life, and we can say that the more the dream ignores the logic of waking life, the more it exemplifies the circumstances in which the instincts exist in the id. Incompatibilities and ambiguities are accepted without any sense of their being unusual.

Another parallel to the way instincts irrationally live together in the id is the way in which people often make false associations between the differing experiences they have had. A sick child who has had to go into hospital may associate the unpleasantness of hospital with the unpleasantness of parental punishment; being in hospital (in one important sense) feels the same as being punished. The child may, therefore, ask what he or she has done wrong and why he or she is being punished. This experience of the child, which is more of an automatic reaction than a response based on logic, parallels the kind of false associations and illogicalities that exist in the id.

To the id and ego processes a third type is added. This is the superego, meaning 'over me'. It represents the moral attitudes and values a person holds. These develop early in life through the rewards and punishments administered by the parents.

The superego has two components, the conscience and the ego-ideal. The conscience, concerned essentially with identifying for people what is morally wrong, punishes them with feelings of guilt when they contravene their ethical outlook. The ego-ideal, defining for people what they ought to be, rewards them with a sense of pride when they fulfil their moral aspirations, values and ideals.

The child learns the parent's moral outlook at an early age. Freud regarded the superego as virtually complete by the age of 7 years. He thought of it as rather like a parent who has taken up residence in the personality and is there ready to chastise a person or reward him or her. Since it does not occur to the child, or later the adult, to question this internal parent, the superego may have a lifelong influence. For example, a person who develops a strict moral outlook in childhood may suffer from unnecessarily high levels of guilt throughout life.

Superego and id are generally in opposition to each other. The superego is irrationally obsessed with the difference between right and wrong. It is essentially self-righteous in nature. The id, on the other hand, selfishly and hedonistically seeks the fulfilment of its own desires. It operates by what Freud called the pleasure principle, the principle of always seeking pleasure and avoiding pain.

The opposition between id and superego is normally controlled by the ego, which aims to maintain a balance in the personality. This balance is achieved by satisfying the requirements of superego and id to varying degrees. Differences in the way in which people achieve this balance account for differences in personality between one person and another. These differences emerge mainly during childhood as the psycho-sexual stages Freud described are negotiated (see Chapter 7).

Freud saw the human personality as essentially in conflict. If the id gains the upper hand and overthrows the management functions of the ego, a person loses the rational faculties that enable him or her to distinguish between what is going on inside the personality and what is going on outside. It therefore becomes impossible to distinguish between imagination and reality, and insanity or psychosis results. If the superego gains the upper hand, a person will constantly be troubled, if not disabled, by high levels of guilt and anxiety and will suffer from emotional problems that are often labelled a neurosis.

The relation between levels of functioning and types

Figure 8.1 shows the relationship between the three levels of mental functioning – conscious, preconscious and uncon-scious – and the three types of process at work in the person-ality – id, ego and superego. The id is wholly unconscious. The ego and superego are mainly conscious and preconscious.

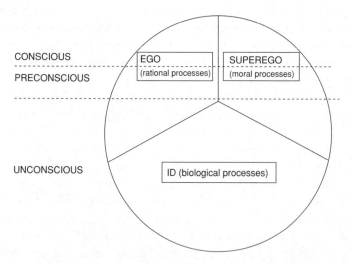

Figure 8.1 Levels and types of process in the personality

What led Freud to his views about personality?

There were a number of influences that led Freud to divide the personality into levels of mental functioning and types of psychological process. Some ideas came from the scientific thinking current when he began his psychological investigations. Other ideas came from analysis of his mentally troubled patients.

A number of Freud's ideas are based on Darwin's theory of evolution. Clearly the instincts in the id operate according to the principles of this theory, selfishly seeking their own survival. Similarly the functioning of the ego can be explained in evolutionary terms. Describing the conscious ego processes as linking inside and outside is a way of answering the question 'What is the evolutionary advantage of conscious awareness?' The fact that the outside world can be represented in the mind along with the representation of the inner psychological world has immense advantages for adaptation and survival, advantages incidentally that go largely unrecognised and are taken for granted.

Another concept current in the scientific climate in which psychoanalytic theory developed was that of energy. Freud became preoccupied with where the personality gains the energy or fuel for its functioning. He concluded that this was derived from biological processes and that there were complex arrangements through which the ego and superego gained what they needed from the id. Little credence is now given to Freud's theory of energy creation and transfer (Fine, 1973). The term libido referring to sexual energy is the only remnant of this theory that continues to be used.

Freud's analytic work with his patients played a significant role in his interest in the unconscious. He was particularly influenced by patients who suffered from a condition known as hysteria. Hysteria is a psychiatric term having a meaning quite different from that in everyday use. Let us look at an example that illustrates its major features.

A secretary who has taken up a new job feels an increasingly strong sense of unease about her work. If she examined this unease (which she does not), she would find it is based on the fact that the letters she types for her boss are fraudulently overcharging her company's customers. These customers are elderly people who in all probability can ill afford to pay more than is necessary. Along with the unease she feels over this is the fact that she receives a very high rate of pay for her work and this rate of pay has made possible a lifestyle that she cannot contemplate giving up. She has therefore what appears to be an insoluble problem. She is unwilling to type fraudulent letters and she is equally unwilling to give up her job.

This problem is ill-defined since she does not wish to face or examine it. However, it does produce progressively more tension. This in turn precipitates a solution, but one determined at an unconscious level. One morning she wakes up to find that her left arm is paralysed. After various medical checks by hospital doctors, no physical basis for this paralysis can be found. Much to her discomfort she is passed on to a psychiatrist. In the course of discussion with her he unearths the connection between the tension her job has been creating and the paralysis she is now suffering from. The arm that was necessary for typing letters now fulfils the function of preventing letters being typed. The mental conflict associated with her work has expressed itself in a physical form.

This example can be used to illustrate three features of hysteria. First, the symptoms fulfil a purpose, in this case the resolution of a conflict. Second, they are produced by a series of processes in the personality about which a person knows little or nothing; that is, the symptoms are unconsciously caused. In view of the role of the unconscious in the development of hysteria, it is not surprising that Freud's studies of the condition went hand in hand with the development of psychoanalytic theory and therapy.

A third feature that often accompanies manifestations of hysteria is that the symptoms imitate or mimic what the patient assumes the symptoms should be like. The secretary, who had no accurate knowledge of true paralysis, naturally showed symptoms that from a medical point of view just did not add up – she could not use a keyboard but could engage in certain actions involved in cleaning her home.

Incidentally the symptoms of hysteria may not be as dramatic as a paralysis. They may be as minor as a headache or backache, whose origins could be the need to direct attention away from a problem (like a failing marriage) and/or the need for sympathy and support.

An example of how the personality works: the defence mechanisms

The overall control and management of the personality carried out by the ego may from time to time be threatened by the potent instinctive forces of the id. These forces can threaten to overpower the ego, and in order to cope with this possibility certain psychological ploys come into play to protect the ego. These are called defence mechanisms.

Suppose a person says of a certain event, 'I became so angry that I feared I would lose control of myself.' This statement can be translated into the language of psychoanalysis. In general terms anger is a mild representation of the instinctive animal rage that exists at an unconscious level in the id. This animal rage is potentially so strong that it could overwhelm the rational controlling processes that form the ego; the person fears that he or she will lose control. The danger of being overwhelmed is experienced as anxiety or fear.

In order to avoid anxiety and maintain its controlling function, the ego may protect itself using a variety of defensive manoeuvres or mechanisms. These mechanisms operate at an unconscious level so that a person is not aware that they have come into operation. They occur spontaneously and automatically.

Below are some examples of defence mechanisms and illustrations of their use. These are only a limited sample of a very wide range (Conce and Plutchkin, 1995). Figure 8.2 gives a diagrammatic picture of how they function.

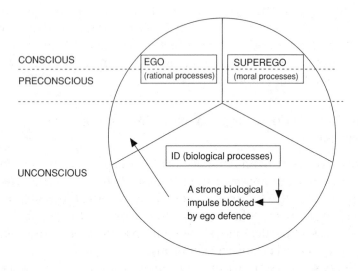

Figure 8.2 The id threatens the ego

1. Repression

A simple way of thinking about repression is to regard it as a means of locking up a motive in the unconscious. To give a more formal definition, in repression, processes threatening to the ego that occur at a conscious and preconscious level become unconscious and those threatening at an unconscious level are made to remain unconscious. The following example of repression describes how an experience that generates anger may then become repressed.

Suppose a person had the following unpleasant experience. He was at a party and an acquaintance somewhat cruelly made fun of him and ridiculed him. This acquaintance caused him to feel humiliated and angry. As he leaves the party he momentarily forgets his anger as he necessarily has to thank his host and hostess. On the way home he experiences a 'nagging feeling at the back of his mind'. Something which he has temporarily forgotten is troubling him.

Now, he may decide not to examine this troublesome feeling; he may refuse to allow it to become clearly defined in consciousness. (Perhaps this incident at the party occurs on a day when a number of unpleasant things have happened to him and he does not want to think about any of them.) As a result the feeling that something unpleasant has happened may slip to an unconscious level, along with the undefined memories and anger it represents. Repression has occurred. If, on the other hand, he *does* allow his memory of this incident and the associated humiliation and anger clear recognition in consciousness but makes a decision not to dwell on them, he is then engaging in suppression. This is a process entirely different from repression, which occurs *unconsciously.*

If, as a result of processes at work in his personality, his experience is repressed, he may well have an amnesia for the whole event. Thus several weeks later, when he meets a friend who had witnessed the unpleasant incident and speaks to him sympathetically about it, he finds that he has little or no memory of it, only a vague, dreamlike, hazy impression.

Repression of memories and emotions is seldom complete. Anger that through repression is 'bottled up' in the unconscious may 'leak' out into thought and behaviour in disguised forms. It still tries to express itself. Thus after being humiliated at a party and having an amnesia for what happened, the next time this man meets the person who did this to him, he angrily criticises him at the slightest provocation and resorts again and again to unprovoked sarcasm. He is not able to recognise the true origins of his aggression and he is not able to perceive that his reactions are irrationally excessive.

Although repression can protect the ego from strong id forces, it does create some problems for the ego. As has just been seen it can hide the real motives a person has, and this can make it difficult for the ego to integrate and control psychological functions.

Here is another illustration of repression, which in principle describes a series of events similar to those reported by

Cameron and Magaret (1951). A man, Arnold, is wandering around a supermarket with his girlfriend to whom he has just become engaged. Another man who appears to be a stranger approaches him and begins to ask him questions that clearly indicate that this man knows or has known him well. He, however, has not the slightest idea who this man is. While he tries to recall this apparent stranger's identity, he turns to his girlfriend and begins to introduce her only to find that he cannot now remember her name.

Some years previous to this incident, Arnold and this man were close friends. While working abroad Arnold met someone, became engaged and, on returning home, introduced her to his friend. Unfortunately for him, his friend and fiancée got on so well together that she broke off her engagement and married the friend. Now in the supermarket Arnold and this friend meet again. Arnold has a complete amnesia for this man's identity, and other unconscious processes block the recall of his present fiancee's name and consequently prevent the possibility of her being introduced to his former friend.

2. Projection

In projection the ego deals with an unacceptable motive by attributing it to someone else. Thus a danger that exists inside the personality is transformed into one that is external, existing in other people. This makes it less threatening.

Let us take as an example of projection the case of a celibate clergyman who from his childhood has regarded sexuality as wrong and would be unsettled if he recognised or tried to come to terms with the potent sexual impulses that are part of his personality. He may resolve this psychological difficulty by regularly assuming that other people are promiscuous and always condemning them. (Clearly not every clergyman who condemns promiscuity is engaging in projection. If, however, sexual sins are an inevitable feature of every sermon, to the neglect of other social evils or Christian exhortation, the suspicions of his congregation may well be justified.)

Projection is a means of disguising a source of psychological conflict. In simple terms what people cannot accept in themselves, they condemn in others. As a result they are able to attribute good characteristics to themselves and bad characteristics to others.

Sometimes a person involved in the use of projection receives some satisfaction from suspicions that someone else is indulging in the forbidden behaviour. The clergyman just referred to may enjoy highly imaginative scenes of others behaving promiscuously while at the same time condemning such behaviour. Alternatively he may feel frustrated by believing that some people satisfy the sexual desires he cannot.

The way relationships work often provides a basis for projection. When we are with another person we are often aware that what we will reveal of ourselves is influenced by the kind of person this is. We are less aware of the fact that what another person reveals is affected by the kind of person we are. Thus often when we describe another individual's personality, we are not so much describing what he or she is like as making statements about how well or badly our relationship is progressing and, by implication, how well or badly the other person is getting on with us. This is a situation that is ripe for projection. A mother who handles her teenage daughter badly and makes a very superficial relationship with her accuses her daughter of being shallow. Actually it is the mother who lacks the capacity to make anything other than a superficial relationship with her daughter and because of this creates the conditions for her daughter's apparently shallow behaviour. She now criticises her daughter for something that, were she to face up it, she would find an unacceptable feature of her own personality.

3. Reaction formation

This involves the ego transforming a motive so that its opposite appears in consciousness. We might observe a teacher giving effusive care and attention to a child who indulges in particularly unpleasant and disruptive behaviour. She does this because her ego is threatened by the very strong, aggressive feelings that the child inspires. Her largely artificial concern for the child counteracts and hides the aggressive feelings operating at a deeper level in her personality. In reaction formation psychological processes 'react' to what is going on deep in the personality by producing the reverse in conscious awareness.

This defence mechanism often occurs in situations where one person is ambivalent about another, having sometimes positive feelings about him or her, sometimes negative. This defence mechanism comes into operation when only the positive side of this ambivalence is emphasised in inflexible and effusive behaviour. This may well irritate the person who is the focus of this behaviour, and, it has been suggested, this irritation may go some way towards satisfying the aggressive feelings of the person involved in reaction formation.

Some mental health patients who suffer from gross suspicion or paranoia may constantly complain that various people are talking about them on the radio or on television and that people such as the police are watching their every move. This may be a reaction formation to the undefined fear that *no-one* is interested in them or cares about them.

4. Rationalisation

One way of diverting attention away from a motive's less legitimate origins and aspects is to interpret it in socially acceptable terms. This the ego does by means of rationalisation, a defence mechanism that is more accessible to conscious examination than most. A mother, seeing her teenage son's developing interest in girls and fearing that this will lead to increasing separation from her, insists on him remaining at home every evening. She (rather too strongly) reasons to herself and her son that it is necessary for him to devote himself solely to his studies to ensure his future success.

5. Displacement

When a motive cannot be gratified by a particular object or when gratification is difficult, the motive may be gratified by a substitute object. This transfer from one object to another is known as displacement. A workman is made fun of by his boss who, he fears, may sack him if he retaliates. When he returns home in the evening, he finds fault with his wife and insults her. Here an aggressive motive is inspired by his boss but is not expressed towards that person. Instead it is expressed towards his wife. Incidentally if his wife has the same fear of her husband as he has of his boss, she may then displace her anger towards their children.

Displacement is usually consciously justified by the use of rationalisation. If the workman is asked why he is verbally abusive to his wife, he will interpret his anger in socially acceptable ways, ways which are related to any immediate and often trivial fault he can find with her.

6. Sublimation

Sublimation is a defence mechanism that is very similar to displacement. In sublimation, however, an instinct moves on from one object to another until it is expressed in a way that is wholly acceptable to society. For example, an artist's sexual instincts may eventually be focused in the dispassionate painting of nudes, an activity for which he gains approval by the circles in which he moves. It is through this process of sublimation that, in spite of the powerful animal nature of the id, civilisation can develop.

7. Regression

Regression refers to the reinstatement of attitudes and behaviour that were characteristic of a former stage of development. A return to this stage takes the ego back to a condition of mastery or security. For example, a newly wed woman, in response to the anxieties of her first argument with her husband, goes home to her mother. In doing this she is returning to the security of an earlier phase of her life.

Regression may involve going back to previously used behaviour patterns or it may simply involve the adoption of behaviour patterns that have immature characteristics. Also, recourse to regression may make it possible for a child to move back to an earlier stage and reorganise the control of his or her motives so that, on return to the stage of development from which the child regressed, a better adjustment can be achieved.

8. Fixation

This defence mechanism, like regression, refers mainly to child development and the refusal to move from the security of one stage of development into a more advanced stage. For example, stimulation of the lips and mouth, reminiscent of infant feeding, may persist throughout life in other forms – chewing, kissing and smoking.

Two features of the use of defence

Foulds (1965) has identified two important features of the use of defence mechanisms. First, he has pointed to the fact that a person involved in defence expresses a level of emotion that is inappropriate. In short, given the circumstances there is too much or too little of the emotion. The earlier example of displacement (where the workman's aggression was displaced to his wife) illustrates the existence of too much emotion; whatever the husband's excuse for criticising his wife, his anger will be found to be excessive.

In contrast to this there are occasions when the use of defence is indicated by too little emotion. As we have seen, a person's dislike and aggressive feelings towards a second person may be constantly masked by the effusive care and concern of a reaction formation; when this second person does something that should make the first genuinely angry, the first person reacts with unnatural calmness.

A second feature of the use of defence mechanisms identified by Foulds concerns the way they generate or cause a person's behaviour without that person being aware of its origins. In other words the use of a defence mechanism involves a motive that is located outside conscious awareness. Again using the example of displacement, the aggressive workman is not aware of the real motive for verbally abusing his wife; that is, he does not know that he is abusing her because his boss made him feel aggressive. He is unable to detect or explain his true motives because his use of displacement is unconscious and automatic. Thus if he could be totally honest (and he isn't because he is resorting to rationalisation), he would find that his behaviour was a total mystery to him. If his aggression were in reality fully justified, he could answer the question, 'Why am I reacting in this way?' with sane, realistic and 'wholesome' answers.

If then a person uses a defence mechanism, some of his behaviour is controlled not by conscious but by unconscious processes. It follows that if a lot of defence mechanisms are being used, then more and more of behaviour is determined outside awareness.

If a person's experience indicates that he or she is not the manager of behaviour, a conclusion may be drawn that some other individual or thing is in control. Thus it is not unusual to find among the mentally disordered those who complain that they are being controlled by unseen people or machines. Their use of defence mechanisms has made them observers but not controllers of their own behaviour.

SOME BASIC THEMES IN PSYCHOANALYSIS AND LINKS WITH THE INTRODUCTION

Basic themes in Part II

In the first chapter in this section, we looked at some of the principles of psychoanalytic therapy. Early in this chapter there was a description of a client, Jim, whose problems were used to illustrate the influence his early history had on him. The following chapter began from a similar starting point describing the personal history of Clare.

In principle there are many parallels between the effect their respective families had on Jim and Clare. Also, Jim's personal history could be analysed using many of the ideas in Chapter 6 on self-analysis, as could Clare's using many of the ideas in Chapter 5 on therapy. For example, there are several identifiable neurotic trends in Jim's personality. They have a number of causes and manifestations and have important relations with each other within his personality. Clare's problems can easily be seen as giving rise to transference reactions; she tries to please everyone with whom she has a relationship, just as she had pleased her mother.

In Freud's mind there were links between his theory of child development and his personality theory. As pointed out in Chapter 8, id processes are present at birth but ego and superego develop during the child's early years. Freud regarded the events of the Oedipal period as particularly important in the development of the superego. He thought that a boy's identification with his father not only resolved the Oedipus complex but also led to the completion of the superego.

Incidentally, as suggested in Chapter 5, a therapist using the traditional view represented in the 'sexual' stages described by Freud will analyse events differently from an object relations theorist. Also since, in general terms, therapy is concerned with strengthening ego processes, differences of view about what has caused unconscious problems in childhood will affect how this strengthening is to be achieved. An analyst holding an orthodox Freudian view might, for instance, focus on Oedipal conflicts in order to resolve transference problems.

The point was also made in Chapter 5 that a difficulty for the therapist is to know who is putting what into the ongoing process of therapy. This difficulty also arises in ordinary relationships with the use of the defence mechanisms described in Chapter 8. Such use disguises the nature and origins of motivation and neither the person subject to a defence mechanism nor the individual who has to deal with him or her is in a position to know exactly why things are happening as they are.

Psychoanalytic thinking and the change process

As we have seen psychoanalytic schools of thought use interpretation to link both unconscious processes and personal history. Since personal history is unchangeable, why should an understanding of it have therapeutic effects?

One possible answer to this question is as follows. Customarily a person is in the grip of certain psychological processes intimately connected with his or her past and which are unrecognised and therefore not understood. This lack of recognition and understanding prevents the development of realistic attitudes.

Whenever thoughts, feelings or behaviour are related to their historical origins, the manner in which history produced them is made clear. This makes them more open to examination. Moreover when the assumptions (unconsciously made) that surround thoughts, feelings and ways of relating to others are exposed, a person can be released from their influence. As Keeney (1983) has pointed out, once an unconscious assumption is made explicit, it can no longer function as it has done in the past.

The historical and social context of psychoanalysis

We have seen in Chapter 8 how Freud developed his theory from the ideas current in the science of his day. This biased his thinking, particularly towards overestimating the importance of the biological and underestimating the influence of the social. For example, he regarded a person's sexuality as essentially a set of biological processes and did not take sufficient note of the fact that the meaning a person attributes to sexual experience is shaped by the society to which he or she belongs (Fromm, 1982); some may have learned to regard their sexual impulses as a form of appetite, a hunger to be satisfied; others may regard it as the means of expressing intimacy, love and commitment.

The apparently objective language of psychoanalysis often masks the influence of assumptions derived from the context in which it developed. A pattern of behaviour can be described in English, French or German or described in psychoanalytic terminology. Clearly all of these are descriptions, but the last may appear to be an explanation. Freud's view of women is certainly open to this criticism; in large measure he took his own personal attitudes to women, determined by where he was located historically and socially, translated them into the apparently objective terms of his theory and passed them off as an explanation of female psychology.

It has been rather scathingly suggested that the only personality we can learn about by reading Freud's theory of personality is Freud's. With this in mind it is instructive to read Trilling and Markus' (1964) *The Life and Work of Sigmund Freud*. Here one learns, for example, that Freud was nearer to his mother in age than his mother was to his father. This throws some light on his preoccupation with the Oedipus complex and the importance he attached to it. In addition to examining the relation between Freud's experience and his theoretical ideas, one can usefully analyse his personal history using the principles of psychoanalysis (Chapter 5) and self-analysis (Chapter 6).

To some extent more recent developments in psychoanalysis have offset some of the criticisms made here of Freud's views. Not all psychoanalysts, however, have been free to criticise the founder of psychoanalysis.

FURTHER READING

On psychoanalytic therapy

1. Bugental, J.F.T. (1976) *The Search for Existential Identity.* San Francisco: Jossey-Bass.

This is not a book about psychoanalytic therapy but it does describe the kinds of fundamental change that take place in long-term therapy. It is a collection of case histories rather than a book about therapeutic techniques. These histories, particularly those beyond the first one or two, indicate some fascinating differences in clients and the changes that they can undergo.

2. Casement, P. (1985) *On Learning from the Patient.* London: Tavistock Publications.

This is a brilliant book. It describes how, during therapy, Casement slips easily from a sympathetic analysis of what the patient has said and the part he has played in this to an analysis of his own feelings about the patient and how he should react. This demonstrates to a startling degree the way psychoanalytic concepts work.

Casement has written another book, *Further Learning from the Patient,* which is also well worth reading (published in 1990 by Tavistock Publications).

On self-analysis

1. Horney, K. (1942) *Self-analysis*. London: Kegan Paul, Trench, Trubner. Recently republished by Norton.

This is a readable book and clearly one which will develop further the reader's understanding of the chapter on self-analysis. It can usefully be read in conjunction with Bugental's book, either before or after.

On object relations theory

1. Cashdan, S. (1988) *Object Relations Therapy*. London: Norton.

This is a well-written introduction to object relations theory and an application of its principles to adults in therapy.

2. Eichenbaum, L. and Orbach, S. (1984) *What Do Women Want*. London: Fontana.

This book and Lillian Rubin's below combine interests in object relations theory with differences in the development of girls and boys. Both books are aimed predominantly at a female readership. In addition to analysing the experiences of women, they also describe the problems that arise in adult relationships as a result of the psychological differences between men and women.

3. Rubin, L. (1985) *Intimate Strangers*. London: Fontana.

On defence mechanisms

1. Freud, A. (1936) *The Ego and the Mechanisms of Defence*. London: Hogarth Press and the Institute of Psychoanalysis.

This is an important book on the defence mechanisms and will familiarise the reader with psychoanalytic concepts.

On the life of Freud

1. Trilling, L. and Markus, S. (Eds.) (1964) *The Life and Work of Sigmund Freud.* Harmondsworth: Penguin Books.

This is an edited and abridged version of Jones' *Life and Work of Sigmund Freud.* As already suggested, the reader may find it a useful exercise to examine Freud's ideas about childhood and personality in the light of what this book reveals of his own childhood and personality.

PART III

INTRODUCTION TO BEHAVIOURISM

In the years following the turn of the century, psychologists became increasingly envious of the rapid growth in scientific knowledge. Subjects such as physics, chemistry and biology, and applied forms of these sciences such as engineering and medicine, were continually making startling advances. As a result of their envy some psychologists suggested that if psychology modelled itself on the objectivity of other sciences, it would achieve the same kind of success.

Watson (1913) crystallised this desire for objectivity when he suggested that since behaviour is the only aspect of an individual's psychology that is open to observation and scrutiny, behaviour alone should be the focus of study. Concepts such as 'thought', 'feeling' or 'the mind' should not be included in the science of psychology since they cannot be observed or measured. It is this emphasis on behaviour to the exclusion of what are customarily regarded as important psychological processes that lies behind the term 'behaviourism'.

The first 50 years of behaviourism had three main strands: experimental work with animals, a preoccupation with how learning takes place and the relationship between learning and reward. The first of these, work with animals, was carried out acknowledging that an animal is less complicated than a human being and is therefore a more appropriate subject with which to start. The rat was the animal most frequently used since rats bred quickly and, as a consequence, were a ready source of new experimental subjects.

The process of learning was seen as central to understanding behaviour. Watson's view, for example, was that all behaviour was learned. The actions of a problem child or the symptoms of mental disorder were learned in the same way as more appropriate behaviour. Therefore making sense of the nature of learning, initially through animal experimentation, became extremely important.

Learning was generally regarded as taking place in response to reward, and behaviourists have a great deal to say about how rewards work. They also have a great deal to say about how rewards can be used to change problematic behaviour.

These early and dominant traditions in behaviourism, emphasising the importance of the study of behaviour alone, animal experimentation, learning and reward, are represented in the fourth chapter of this section, 'The experimental foundations of behaviourism', and to some extent in the second and third chapters on personal change and children.

Over the past 25 years behaviourists have taken an increasingly sympathetic approach to including in their brand of psychology processes that occur inside an individual, processes that are not as accessible to observation as is behaviour. Several trends have combined to produce this change, one of the most significant of which has been the discovery that a person can reproduce the behaviour of a model a long time after having witnessed what that model has done. This, of course, is proof of the presence of some kind of internal process.

This change in behaviourist thinking has provided the basis for a number of developments. One of these is cognitive therapy. This form of therapy is explained in the first chapter in this section.

9 COGNITIVE THERAPY

SUMMARY

Cognitive therapists believe that understanding the link between an event, its interpretation and the emotions that follow it is an important key to resolving emotional difficulties.

They also believe that, depending on how realistically or otherwise incidents or events are interpreted, there are two broad categories of emotion; there are emotions that are easy to cope with and that generally promote productive behaviour, and there are emotions that are extreme, difficult to manage and that block productive behaviour.

In what follows the way in which cognitive therapists expose the link between thought and emotion is explained, along with the methods they use for changing thought, emotions and behaviour.

Introduction

There are a number of cognitive approaches to psychotherapy (Dryden and Golden, 1986). What follows draws on the work of Beck (Beck, *et al.*, 1979) and Ellis (1979), particularly the latter. The term 'cognitive therapy' strictly speaking applies to Beck's work and the term 'rational–emotive therapy' to that of Ellis. I have used the first of these terms to cover ideas drawn from both writers.

The link between thought and emotion

Writing in the first century BC, the Greek philosopher Epictetus stated, 'People are not disturbed by things, but by the view they take of them.' This means that when a person feels that circumstances are making him or her anxious, it is not the circumstances in themselves that are creating the anxiety but the way in which they are being interpreted. In other words, although we all experience the cause of an emotion as lying in an event, what comes between an event and the feelings it generates is an interpretation. If it is the interpretation of an event that creates emotional feelings, it is possible that certain disturbing emotions can be avoided by making sure interpretations are realistic.

Let us look at an incident from therapy that illustrates the link between unrealistic or inappropriate interpretations and unpleasant emotions. A therapist was treating a depressed woman, Barbara, whom he saw each week on a Friday morning. One Friday he asked her, 'How has your week gone since we last met? How, for example, did your day go yesterday?' She replied dejectedly, 'I dropped a pint of milk yesterday.' After a long pause and a heavy sigh she added, 'You see, John, I'm not even capable of picking up a pint of milk now.'

Here are two faulty ways of thinking that were contributing to and were perhaps the root cause of Barbara's depression. The first involves regarding a simple mistake, dropping a pint of milk, as representative of the day's (perhaps even of the week's) events. On the day she had this minor accident Barbara had performed literally hundreds of successful acts, but none of these were recalled or regarded as significant.

The second faulty way of thinking involves regarding what happened as representative of her personality. In saying that she could not now pick up a pint of milk without dropping it, she was telling the therapist that she was totally incompetent and therefore useless and worthless.

These two faulty ways of thinking are related to each other. No doubt, because of her depressed mood, Barbara tended to focus on one kind of event rather than another. She picked out one unsuccessful act while ignoring all others. Having only recalled what had gone wrong, she then used this to confirm her feelings of worthlessness. Once her feelings were confirmed, she became even more sensitive to mistakes and failures and even more depressed.

Useful and counterproductive emotions

Attitudes to mistakes, such as dropping a pint of milk, can generate two kinds of emotion. One kind is exemplified in such emotions as regret, sorrow, frustration or annoyance, and the other in more disturbing emotions such as anxiety, depression and rage. The first kind can motivate productive behaviour, which can lead to the eventual fulfilment of a person's goals, wishes and preferences. The second kind of emotion tends to have a disabling effect on the individual and invariably blocks effective action. It prevents a person from fulfilling any productive goals and originates from the kinds of thought pattern that we have seen at work in Barbara, who was seriously depressed.

Many people who suffer extreme emotions go on to indulge in behaviour that is not in their best interests – withdrawal, procrastination, unjustified dependence on others, substance abuse and so on. Barbara had a highly developed sense of self-pity, an overdependence on others and a tendency to manipulate them into feeling sorry for her.

The faulty thoughts and the self-defeating conclusions that Barbara drew from them are not unusual, nor are several other patterns of thought that give rise to extremes of emotion that are counterproductive. We will look at six types.

Mistaking a preference for a need

People very often mistake what is essentially a preference for a need. One of the aims of the advertising industry is to promote this kind of thinking. A person may, as a result of reading an advertisement, regard him or herself as 'needing' an expensive car, a Jaguar or Rolls Royce. If this 'need' is taken seriously and cannot be satisfied, it can create unbearable levels of frustration. A person will think, 'I need this but I cannot afford it... but I really need it!'

Although people sometimes may be troubled by their 'needs' for certain material possessions, examples of mistaking a need for a preference are more often found in areas such as the 'need' for success, pleasure and justice. The last of these, the 'need' for justice, is a frequent problem. Many people regard this as so important that they demand that they be treated completely fairly. If even a relatively trivial incident occurs in which they are treated unfairly, they can become emotionally disturbed. They cannot 'get the incident out of their minds', dwelling interminably on what happened to them.

No-one can go through life without at some time being treated unjustly. It is wise to recognise this and to substitute, 'I prefer to be treated justly' for 'I need to be treated justly.' Not only will this produce less extreme and more manageable emotions but it will also produce, in behaviour, a more realistic approach to the problem. These benefits also apply to substituting 'I prefer a Rolls Royce' for 'I need a Rolls Royce.'

Using words like 'must', 'ought' and 'should'

Similar to the effect of mistaking a need for a preference is the use of such words as 'must', 'ought' and 'should'. People often use these words to try to motivate what they do, but they only end up making impossible demands on themselves. They say things like, 'I "must" or "should" always be successful at those things that are important to me, otherwise I can have no respect for myself.'

Demands may not only be made on self by using words such as 'must', 'ought' and 'should' but may also be made on reality. A person may erroneously say, 'I must, I ought to, I should be treated justly at all times' or 'My world must or should at all

times be a just place and I will get very upset' – to the point of
mental disturbance – 'if it proves not to be'. This is often
followed up by statements that indicate how catastrophic it is if
the world is not as it 'ought' to be. 'If I am not treated justly this
is catastrophic and I cannot stand it!' Again, saying these
things creates unjustified emotional turmoil.

There are important questions that can be used to challenge
words like 'must', 'ought', 'should' and 'catastrophic' and
phrases such as 'I cannot stand this'. These include questions
like the following: 'Why do I think like this?' 'Who says it is a
case of "must", "should", "ought", "catastrophic" and "I
cannot stand it"?' 'What evidence is there that things are as I
imply?' In view of the emotional trauma involved; it is sensible
to question and challenge the use of these words.

Mistaking desires for demands

Sometimes making demands on reality takes the form of esca-
lating a desire into a requirement that must be fulfilled – 'I
must get what I want; I must get it because I want it' or a
response that often happens in therapy, 'I demand that
changing the way I think be easy'. It is, of course, illogical to
suggest that I will get what I want merely by wanting it.
Making this kind of mental demand on reality is again usually
accompanied by unfortunate emotional consequences.

If desires experienced as demands are not fulfilled, a person
may feel angry and frustrated, and this may be channelled in
various directions, condemning him or herself, others or the
world. This condemnation, if not actually counterproductive,
often proves to be pointless.

Rating self in terms of one characteristic

A person who, like Barbara, regards a mistake as representative
of his or her personality usually expresses this in terms of an
all-embracing, derogatory self-evaluation. The conclusion is

drawn, 'Since I've made a mistake, I'm useless', or 'I'm a fool.' Underlying these statements is the belief, 'I have the personality of a mistake-maker.'

Apart from the disturbing emotional consequences of this for self, this attitude has other problems inherent in it. For a start its logic is at fault. If a person is a fool, it follows that all a person's acts must be foolish. It also follows that everything else that is known about a person should be ignored since the descriptive word 'fool' can be regarded as summarising his or her personality. However, a person is too complicated a being to be described by any one single word.

Questioning the logic of self-rating in terms of a single word or category provides one antidote to the problems associated with it. Another is to learn to evaluate only one's *acts* or *thoughts*. Evaluating these not only eliminates self-rating and its consequences but also makes it easier for a person to change. If I say that I am a fool, the implication is that it is in my nature to be a fool, and my nature is something that is impossible to change. If, however, I say that I have done something foolish (or have thought something foolish), the implication is that I can choose to behave (or think) differently.

Self-acceptance is a process that cognitive therapists seek to foster since it leads to more wholesome feelings than does self-evaluation. Doing something wrong or making a mistake does not prove that everything about a person is foolish or bad, and self-acceptance is a much better basis for producing change than is self-condemnation.

Perfectionist thinking

Yet another example of a faulty mental habit is that of perfectionist thinking: 'I did badly because 5 per cent of what I did was not right.' A very short step from this kind of thinking is to have one's mind wholly filled with everything that is less than perfect. This in turn leads on to the belief that there is no value in anything that one does.

Often coupled with perfectionism are judgments made in an all-or-nothing fashion; that is, 'Getting it 95 per cent right is the same as getting it totally wrong.' If you think like this, having aimed at a certain idealistic goal, you will regard yourself as a total failure when your activities fall short of perfection.

Often accompanying this pattern of thought, which results in depressed feelings and low self-esteem, is the tendency to discount what has been good about your performance. This is sometimes seen in the steps of recovery from a period of mental problems such as anxiety or depression.

Barbara demonstrated this tendency to discount evidence of progress. During her depression she had spent long periods of time marooned at home so that friends and relatives had had to do her shopping for her. One of the first signs of recovery was her visiting her local shop. When some of her friends pointed to this as a sign of progress, she complained that she could only stay in the shop long enough to get what she wanted but before her depression she would have been happy to stay chatting to the shopkeeper and to the other customers. To give another example, when she first came to the hospital in her car, not having driven for several months, her therapist mentioned this as a sign of progress. Yet again she complained that it was a 'mammoth' effort for her to start using her car again and that there was a time when she could have driven anywhere 'at the drop of a hat.'

Although there is truth in what she said about both shopping and driving, these statements show how Barbara was judging her behaviour by what were, at that time, near-unattainable standards. These standards prevented her from taking any encouragement from her progress and acted to reinforce her depression. Discounting successes meant that no advantage accrued from any step towards recovery. Barbara's therapist pointed out that recognition of any small improvement could and would motivate further progress.

Incidentally rating oneself in terms of one characteristic, as described above, is often linked to demandingly perfectionist attitudes – 'If I cannot produce a perfect performance then I am hopeless and useless.'

Inflated emotions generated by attitudes to problems

Sometimes a client's reaction to a problem will prove to be more problematic than the problem itself. Barbara, for example, had a bad memory and had difficulty remembering appointments, what items of shopping needed to be bought and so on. This failure to remember is regrettable and requires her, if life is to carry on reasonably smoothly, to keep a record of appointments and make shopping lists. A person with this problem can, however, worry about having a bad memory, and this worry becomes progressively more exaggerated and inflated. Anxieties about this problem then pose greater difficulties than does the problem itself.

There are several examples of this process. People can be depressed about their depression, highly anxious about their panic attacks and guilty and ashamed of their anger. Sometimes these secondary problems, such as anxiety about panic attacks, must be recognised and addressed before the primary ones (the panic attacks themselves) can be dealt with.

Simply distinguishing between the problem and a person's reaction to it is sometimes sufficient for him or her to react more realistically. Another solution to this difficulty is to discuss the primary problem in a way that underlines its real size. This kind of discussion will reduce the magnitude of a person's reaction to the problem and may well lead to more sensible ways of handling it.

The origins of faulty patterns of thought

Many of the ways of thinking described above have developed in childhood (Ellis and Bernard, 1983). Parents and other adults often provide a model of how to think and feel about circumstances and self. The following, which describes a fairly common sequence of events, provides one illustration of how a parent's reactions to a child's misdemeanours lead to the development of faulty ways of thinking.

Suppose a child says something objectionable, is disobedient or breaks a rule made by parents. The parent may then convey through what is said and the tone with which it is said, 'You must be good all the time.' This encourages the child to engage in perfectionist thinking. The parent goes on, 'You – not just your words or behaviour but you, yourself – are awful, horrible and bad.' The implication here is that the child should rate him or herself in terms of certain characteristics.

Further implications may lie in what follows. 'I can't stand it when you do such things. You deserve to be severely punished.' In response to the parent's reaction, the child adopts the same thoughts as the parent, makes the same attributions to self as the parents have made and then suffers from the unfortunate emotional consequences of such thoughts and attributions. He or she picks up the same way of thinking and reasons, 'When I have done something wrong I am awful, horrible and bad and I deserve to feel worthless.'

The parent could adopt an alternative approach to the child's misdemeanours. The parent could identify the undesirable behaviour clearly and specifically. He or she might convey the following sentiments, 'I regret that you've done this and would prefer you to behave differently. However, I continue to respect you even though I'm unhappy about the way you've just behaved.'

In addition to modelling a more realistic thought pattern for the child, there is another feature of this kind of communication that recommends it. By specifying the problematic behaviour of the child, the parent implies that the child could have behaved differently. This contrasts with communicating that there is something wrong with the child's personality by describing him or her as 'insolent', 'lazy' or 'careless.' Changing a personality characteristic is well-nigh impossible whereas changing behaviour is often well within his or her capabilities. This principle of fostering change by identifying behaviour rather than personality characteristics is similar to one mentioned earlier in this chapter; a person is more likely to change as a result of evaluating thoughts and behaviour than by making global evaluations of self.

Explaining thought patterns and their consequences

Since faulty thought patterns and ways of interpreting events can cause problematic emotions without a person realising it, a possible first step in therapy is to explain this. With some clients a cognitive therapist will explain the relation between thought and emotion using a diagram. 'A' is described as an activating event that triggers 'C' an emotional consequence. Between 'A' and 'C' comes 'B', a belief, which is a primary source of the emotion at 'C.' The validity of this belief may need to be questioned by disputing it at 'D.'

Many of the faulty thought patterns that have been identified above, that interpose themselves between an event and the experience of a subsequent emotion, occur in the form of words that a person says to him or herself. The existence and nature of this self-talk can be brought to the client's attention. The client can learn to ask, whenever a strong or extreme, unpleasant emotion is experienced, 'What am I saying to myself? Since I'm experiencing a disturbing emotion, what words are going through my mind?'

The therapist is often in a privileged position when it comes to understanding the kind of internal dialogue that goes on in the client. He or she has a good working knowledge of the general forms that erroneous self-talk can take. The therapist can easily apply this knowledge to specific problems.

Let us look at one possible way of explaining these processes. This example describes the form of explanation given to Barbara early in therapy. You will recall that she had regarded dropping a pint of milk as a summary of her life and personality. If I were a therapist and speaking from the point of view of a fallible human being, I could point out to Barbara that I too made mistakes but I neither regarded these as representing the totality of my daily life nor considered them as wholly representative of my personality. If I did both of these things, I would suffer the same emotional consequence as she did – depression.

I could further point out that an essential difference between her being depressed and my not being so was brought about by our differing thought patterns. I too would be depressed if I developed the same mental habits that she had. Suppose, for example, at the end of each day I select those aspects of my work that I had not done well, along with any mistakes I had made. I then set myself the task of thinking about these for 20 minutes or so. The first consequence of this would be that at the end of this period I would be depressed. This is because, when I think in a certain way, certain feelings follow.

A second consequence is that after a week or so I would develop a facility for having depressing thoughts. Spontaneously things I had done badly and mistakes I had made long ago would come to mind, and this would happen not only in the 20-minute period set aside for this but in other moments during the day when I was relaxing or day-dreaming. The habit of thinking about my poor performance and the mistakes I made would have become more automatic and less under my control. It is as if the habit begins to have an independent life of its own. The more practice Barbara had at selecting certain events and interpreting them in a certain way, the easier it was to develop a depressed approach to everything. In fact this type of thinking eventually became so spontaneous that it led to her regarding herself as obviously or self-evidently worthless.

Barbara, incidentally, was involved in a good example of the tendency to dwell on past mistakes. She had once, at the suggestion of one of her relatives, threatened her 21-year-old son (who was living at home) with expulsion unless he did more of what she wanted. This proved to be a serious error of judgement since he used her threat as an excuse to leave home. She dwelt a great deal on this mistake and it occupied her mind for many fruitless hours. An error like this, however, no matter how serious it proved to be, did not constitute grounds for her concluding she was worthless. Fallible human beings make small and sometimes large mistakes.

Resistance to changing thought patterns

If clients understand the explanations given by the therapist, they will understand the role that their own thinking plays in creating their emotional disturbance. Sometimes analysing what is happening in terms of 'A', 'B', 'C' and 'D' can have a startling affect on the client, with the virtual disappearance of his or her mental and emotional problems in a matter of minutes or even seconds. Unfortunately this is not always the case. Many clients have to come to the realisation that, after years of having easily and naturally adopted certain ways of thinking, change will not take place without concentrated effort.

Such effort is often resisted. The client's 'need' to be comfortable at all times and to do what comes naturally prevents actively changing those self-statements that are problematic. The client may demand that the therapist provides the kind of help that makes change easy, and it is 'awful' or 'catastrophic' if he or she does not. These thought processes will not easily change and many clients resist working things out mentally in a way that would take them from disastrous ways of thinking to ways that are more rational and more in tune with reality.

Because the client has practised using faulty patterns of thought, there is a tendency on his or her part to hold on to these patterns and, even when they have been discovered, to return to them in a process that is essentially one of 'reindoctrination'; a person's upset continues because there is a constant and regular return to using the same kinds of interpretation and belief over and over again. The client, therefore, must conduct a ruthless, hard-headed campaign. He or she must recognise that it can be very difficult to give up even the most inefficient habits that have been thoroughly learned and practised. For this reason several methods may have to be used to help the client.

Methods of change

A wide range of methods is used in cognitive therapy. We have already looked at antidotes to the six faulty thought patterns. We have also looked at the role of explanation. Other methods include exchanging client and therapist roles and encouraging the client, each day in a 'homework assignment', to record and analyse disturbed emotions and unproductive behaviour.

A method that forces the client to dispute certain thought patterns is to reverse the roles of client and therapist. Once an explanation has been given by the therapist, both the understanding and effectiveness of this explanation can be tested by asking the client to take the therapist's role. The therapist, meanwhile, takes the client's role and repeats the kinds of statement the client has made.

Thus, having explained the relation between events and emotions and having explained the particular ways in which Barbara's thinking was at fault, I might say, 'Look Barbara, I've just come into the hospital and you as therapist have said to me, "How has your week gone? How, for example, did you get on yesterday?". In reply I say, "Yesterday I dropped a pint of milk. You see, Barbara, I can't even pick up a pint of milk now without dropping it". I would then go on to say to Barbara, 'How would you, as the therapist, respond to this?'

Clearly if she has understood what has been explained to her, she can, as therapist, deal with my problematic patterns of thought. Not only will she be able to deal with these but also in doing so she will be attacking what is erroneous in her own thinking by pointing out to me, as the would-be client, what is wrong with my thinking.

Since it is important for the client to work outside the therapy sessions, the therapist may set the client 'homework assignments.' One example of a homework assignment is to record situations and instances that give rise to disturbed emotions or are associated with unproductive behaviour. Each of these situations will be found to be associated with a certain train of thought. Once this association is recognised further analysis can take place based on the kind of questions already referred to – 'What am I saying to myself?', 'What is the evidence for taking this view?' and so on. The client can then write down his or her thoughts and can figure out and practise those thoughts that lead to more productive emotions and behaviour.

The use of humour

Humour is often used in a number of different ways to supplement the methods described above. A client's ideas can be taken to extremes or reduced to absurdity – 'Because of the mistakes you have made you regard yourself as a fool. This is a label or role that you will find very hard to live up to. Can you really make *everything* you do look silly?'

Various instructions may be given which highlight what the client is thinking. A tutor, for example, gave the following instructions to one of her students who was anxious about essay writing. Knowing about cognitive therapy, she suspected that this student was indulging in certain counterproductive ways of thinking. As she wished to expose these, she suggested he might be using one or all of the following five rules:

1. Set an impossibly high standard for yourself – like getting 'A' grades for everything – and, when you fail, castigate yourself for this disaster. Tell yourself you can respect yourself only if you can fulfil your own high standards. Hate yourself for not doing so.

    Occasionally you will come across students who have gained a 'B' or even a 'C' and regard this as a victory over impossible odds. Regard such students as totally misguided.

    Don't set realistic goals for yourself.
2. Regard any grade you get as an indication of the kind of person you are. If you get an 'A' grade, you are an 'A' person, if a 'B' a 'B' person, if a 'C' or a 'D' a write-off – completely useless and worthless.

If you do get an 'A', remind yourself, preferably over and over again, that you will probably fail next time and this will prove that you really are a failure (and everyone will know it). By getting an 'A' a person can actually generate more feelings of anxiety and vulnerability than by getting a lower grade.

Don't regard grades as a form of feedback on your performance. Don't regard them as representing an aspect of your work. Always regard them as representing everything about you.

3. Try and motivate yourself by using words such as 'must', 'ought' and 'should.' For example, you can tell yourself that you 'must', 'ought to' and 'should' get 'A's. These words in themselves provide no real motivation while at the same time creating a great deal of pressure and anxiety. They also make you feel inadequate and guilty when you fail to achieve your goal. When this happens you can regard yourself as a total failure.

Don't view words such as 'must', 'ought' and 'should' with suspicion. Don't challenge this way of thinking by asking, 'Who says I "must", "ought" or "should"?'

4. Always bear in mind the negative comments that were made on your last essay. Dwell on them and let them depress you.

Don't regard negative comments as a useful form of feedback. Don't recall any positive comments that were made or let positive comments become a realistic part of your thinking.

5. Conclude that the anxious and negative feelings you have are a reflection of the way things are. Conclude that your situation cannot be changed, that it is hopeless and that you are a loser.

Don't regard your feelings as having come from the way you think about your situation. Do not say, 'The way I am thinking is generating my feelings of anxiety and depression'.

Ellis (1993), who advocates the use of humour, has composed a number of humorous songs incorporating the principles of cognitive therapy. He reports some very good results for those of his clients who regularly sing these songs to themselves.

Although cognitive therapists use humour to make fun of human behaviour or ideas, they are careful never to ridicule a client. Care must be taken with the use of humour, and in fact with other aspects of therapy, since certain depressed clients may be so practised in interpreting the world in a self-defeating manner that they can do this with any and every intervention by the therapist. The therapist must check that the client is attacking faulty thoughts and not berating him or herself for having them. A therapist who, for example, points out to a client that rating him or herself in terms of a single character-istic is foolish may find the client saying dejectedly, 'What a fool I am for rating myself in this way!'

Barbara's therapist on one occasion listened to her reel off a list of her faults. Wishing to discuss the problems posed by her attitudes to herself, he said in a perfectly neutral tone of voice, 'You seem to be very self-critical'. Despondent Barbara replied, 'And I'm self-critical too'. Here with consummate ease she interprets feedback that is intended to be helpful in a way that puts herself down.

Cognitive therapy is not the power of positive thinking

Cognitive therapy does not rely on converting a pessimistic thought into an optimistic one. Rather it involves examining critically a relatively automatic thought pattern that generates emotions that are extreme and difficult to manage. Once this examination has taken place, the client can work at replacing this thought pattern with one that is objectively more reason-able. Persuading a client to remember everything good that has happened to him or her (as in promoting the power of positive thinking) may alter a person's mood for the better but it does not dismantle his or her irrational thinking.

10 THE BEHAVIOURIST APPROACH TO PERSONAL CHANGE

SUMMARY

Some of the reasons for approaching with caution programmes that promise to bring about personal change are given at the beginning of this chapter. The chapter then goes on to look at the relations between personality, circumstances and behaviour.

There are three kinds of changes in behaviour that may be desired: a decrease in unwanted behaviour, an increase in wanted behaviour and a change in emotional reactions. How a person can carry out these changes will be explained.

Certain problems may arise when a person designs his or her own self-change plan. Four of these problems are examined at the end of this chapter.

Introduction

Chapter 6, on self-analysis, was written not necessarily to encourage the reader to engage in self-analysis but primarily to illustrate the relation between present problems and a person's past history. Similarly this chapter is written to illustrate certain behaviourist principles that can be used to change personal habits.

It explains general principles of change. These can be useful but they often need to be supplemented by knowledge about the specific problem to be tackled. If, for example, the reader wishes to change habits such as smoking or overeating, he or she may be well advised to supplement the knowledge gained from this chapter by reading more detailed texts on these subjects.

Some problems posed by self-help programmes

This chapter is similar in approach to many programmes described in self-help books. As with this chapter, one ought to approach such books with caution. Self-help books often give scant regard to the diagnosis of the problem they address and this can have serious consequences. For example, a psychological problem such as depression or anxiety sometimes has physical causes. The thyroid gland embedded in the throat secretes a hormone, thyroxine, which determines the rate at which the cells of the body produce energy. An underactive thyroid can make a person feel apathetic and depressed, and an overactive one can make a person feel irritable and anxious. These conditions require medical treatment. Clearly it is not sensible to treat a form of distress that has a physical basis with a psychological method of change.

Many strategies suggested by self-help books may look feasible but have not been adequately tested. Such testing might show that they are badly designed and, if applied, may result in failure. Some people who follow self-help instructions may not succeed but may go on to blame themselves rather than the method. This can have serious consequences. A depressed person who has followed self-help instructions and failed to improve may see him or herself as being at fault. When this happens it is likely to make the depression worse.

In spite of these problems a self-help programme *can* produce change. It is particularly likely to succeed if it empathically and sympathetically gives a person information about the problem to be tackled and motivates the person to comply with instructions. Motivation is important since many, if not most people, are not sufficiently motivated to persist and successfully complete a programme of change.

No doubt certain abilities and attitudes make success more likely. If, for example, a programme is well within a person's abilities and is applied with the belief that change is possible (Bandura, 1977, 1989), greater success will be achieved than with a programme that is out of step with a person's abilities and applied with a pessimistically fatalistic attitude. Moreover, success is more likely if a person devotes time to the programme and uses a range of methods and strategies. Finally even minimal contact with a person who has specialist knowledge about the problem to be resolved is likely to enhance the chances of success (Rosen, 1982).

Personality traits, behaviour and situations

Most people, in describing themselves or others, use words such as 'aggressive', 'kind', 'obstinate' and 'generous'. They believe that there is something called (say) 'aggression' that exists inside a person. This is regarded as part of his or her personality, and it is this part which generates aggressive behaviour.

An alternative view to this is that an individual's behaviour is caused not so much by personality as by the situation in which it occurs. If we observe aggressive behaviour, we will find that it occurs in some situations but not others. We could take the view that certain conditions 'set off' or 'cue' aggressive behaviour and that situations play a more significant role than does personality.

'Stimulus control' is the technical term for the influence that situations exercise over behaviour. This term suggests that the situation – the stimulus – controls the responses that occur. The concept of stimulus control is based on the belief that the conditions that go to make up a certain situation give rise to the behaviour that is exhibited in it.

Describing a problem in terms of situation or personality

If you attribute any personal problems, such as continually losing your temper, to a personality characteristic, the solutions you look for will be very different from the solutions that come from linking behaviour to situations. Suppose, for example, I describe myself as a nervous person. Describing the problem like this implies that my 'nervousness' is part of my personality. Logically, change is only possible if I become a different person. This, to say the least, will be difficult to accomplish. If I cannot achieve this, I will have to accept that I am 'of a nervous disposition' and will have to organise my life taking this fact into account – a conclusion that is as inevitable as it is pessimistic.

An alternative and radically different approach involves analysing my problem in terms of stimulus control. It is not that I am a nervous person but rather that I engage in nervous behaviour (with its associated feelings and thoughts) in some situations but not in others. In other words my nervousness occurs only under certain conditions.

Obviously it is important to identify precisely what these conditions are. Probably the best way of doing this – and this is something we will be examining in more detail – is for me to keep a diary in which I record details of the situations that are associated with nervous episodes. This record is likely to show that there are a wide range of situations in which I am not nervous. Once I have accumulated a number of descriptions of the situations associated with my nervous behaviour, I can then look at ways of managing them.

Some problems, incidentally, stem not from the existence of the control of situations over behaviour but from a lack of it. A bed, for example, is the place which for most people is associated with sleep. For the insomniac this is not so: bed is associated with being awake, with tossing and turning or sometimes with the intention of going to sleep. In the last instance a person who intends by an act of will to go to sleep is creating a condition that guarantees that sleep will not occur. Sleep in fact results from a combination of relaxation and tiredness. If a person wishes to overcome insomnia, bed must become associated with these in order for sleep to occur. Thus a person should remain in bed only if drowsy and relaxed. If tossing and turning, a person should leave the bed and bedroom to return when in a tired and more quiescent mood. Defeating insomnia like this demonstrates an essential goal of behaviourist self-change – a person must learn to control the conditions that control him or her.

We could regard the range of situations in which a piece of problematic behaviour occurs as a measure of its seriousness. The greater the number of situations associated with the behaviour, the more serious the habit and the more difficult it will be to change. Imagine, for example, a man who lights a cigarette as soon as he wakes in the morning; he smokes while he is shaving and after he has had his breakfast, in the car going to work, at work, during his coffee break and so on. The fact that this behaviour crops up in such a wide range of situations will make it more difficult to change. As we shall see later, one of the first steps in learning to manage his smoking with a view to giving it up is to limit his smoking only to certain situations, such as in the car and at coffee breaks.

Even what we normally accept as positive behaviour will be regarded as problematic if it occurs in too many situations. I am, for example, an affectionate person. Imagine that when I left home this morning I kissed my wife goodbye, at the station I kissed the ticket collector, I embraced the nearest woman on the train ... and so on. Here affectionate behaviour is occurring in too many situations and has obviously become problematic.

In the self-change programme that follows we combine the study of stimulus control and the operation of reward. Such a study makes possible three kinds of change – a decrease in undesirable behaviour, an increase in desirable behaviour and a change in emotional reactions to situations. We will look first at methods used to decrease the frequency of undesirable behaviour.

Decreasing the frequency of undesirable behaviour

Step 1. Identifying behaviour
The first step involves identifying the behaviour a person wishes to change. In the case of something such as smoking, this is easily done. However, if the problem is one that has previously been regarded as a personal characteristic, being aggressive or 'hot-tempered' for example, it must be described or reformulated in terms of behaviour. Thus a person may identify his or her aggression in terms of swearing, shouting, slamming doors and making cutting and sarcastic comments. The aggression, of course, may take a more serious form, such as acts of physical violence.

Step 2. Measuring behaviour
Once behaviour has been identified it can be measured. The next step in the self-change programme is to obtain a measure of the frequency or duration of the behaviour that is to be changed. This is done by recording the amount of problematic behaviour immediately after it occurs. This may involve counting the number of cigarettes smoked per day or the number of cutting or sarcastic statements made.

The daily record should be transferred to a more permanent storage system and, providing this measure of behaviour does not fluctuate wildly, an average per day can be deduced after about a week. This average is known as a baseline.

Studies have shown that amongst smokers who record their behaviour, some 15 per cent 'spontaneously' give up smoking. One possible reason for this is that a significant change takes place when a person becomes an observer of his or her behaviour. When situations set off or cue certain kinds of activities, such as smoking, they are exercising relatively automatic control. When, however, a person becomes an observer of this process, it cannot achieve the same level of control and change becomes possible.

Step 3. Studying antecedents and consequences
While collecting the information necessary for a baseline, there is an opportunity to study aspects of the situation that precede

behaviour – the antecedents – and the changes that result from behaviour – the consequences. Thus recording problematic behaviour (at step 2) should be accompanied by short descriptions of antecedent and consequent conditions. As thoughts and emotions can be part of what takes place before and after behaviour, these should also be noted.

In this stage of a self-change programme, some surprising discoveries can be made, showing how ignorant a person is of the situations that determine behaviour. Let us take overeating as an example.

People who have studied their own overeating with a view to losing weight may discover that they eat not because they are hungry but because they are with friends who are eating; they eat at set times of the day, again whether or not they feel hungry; they eat because they feel depressed or emotionally upset; they miss meals, usually breakfast, and then later eat to excess; they often consume meals too quickly while concentrating on other things such as listening to the radio or watching television; when they prepare a meal they enjoy the equivalent of three meals, one when they sample a little from everything they are preparing, one when they enjoy the meal itself and one when, in clearing up afterwards, they consume the left-overs. By studying their behaviour closely, they realise not only how much food they eat but also that much of their eating behaviour, without their having been aware of it, occurs habitually under set conditions.

Step 4. The management of antecedents
The study of antecedents can contribute not just to an understanding of problematic behaviour but also to its management. We will look at three ways of managing antecedents.

Some authors have suggested a two-stage process. In the first stage a person should avoid the conditions that promote undesirable behaviour. (As will be seen in step 5 a person should reward him or herself for such avoidance.)

In the second stage a person should go through a process of gradual reintroduction to those forms of stimulus control that have their weakest hold on behaviour. After some successes a person can move on to those forms which have a stronger hold. Let us look at an example of this two-stage process.

A man who wished to stop smoking found, in the process of keeping a record of the number of cigarettes he smoked, that stimulus control was exercised by being with friends at work who were smokers. Part of his planned behaviour change, therefore, involved avoidance of such friends or at least the avoidance of such friends in situations that had been habitually associated with smoking. He then reintroduced himself into situations in which he was with his friends, joining them however only for short periods, such as coffee breaks. Later, after rewarding himself for his successes, he joined them for longer periods, such as lunch.

An alternative to avoiding stimulus control is to limit the situations in which it exercises its influence. One woman, described by Watson and Tharp (1977), aimed at narrowing the range of antecedents that was associated with her smoking. She continued to smoke cigarettes but only when she sat in her most uncomfortable chair. After a certain period of time she moved this chair into her cellar, a place that was cold and uninviting. Smoking in this unrewarding situation ultimately resulted in her giving up her the habit altogether.

What this woman had done was to limit the situations that exercised stimulus control to only one. She then altered the character of this situation. The other smoker (referred to above) could also alter the character of the situation that was habitually associated with smoking; he could make friends with nonsmokers (although giving up the relationships with his smoking friends may be something that has too high a cost and that he may not wish to do).

So far we have considered two general ways in which antecedents may be managed, one in which a person avoids situations that set the problematic behaviour in motion (and later goes through a process of gradual reintroduction to those situations) and the other in which a person limits stimulus control to circumstances that are made progressively more unrewarding.

A third way of managing antecedents is to break the chain of events of which they are a part. A person who wishes to lose weight, for example, may know that a chain of events that leads to overeating is missing breakfast and then getting so hungry that it is virtually impossible not to eat to excess. This chain may be interrupted by not missing breakfast. Obviously this prevents the uncontrollable hunger that results.

Again, to take another example from overeating, a person may find that purchases of food items made in a supermarket when hungry are greater in number than those made when not hungry. Buying food is part of the chain of events that leads to overeating. Buying food when not hungry is there-fore advisable.

Step 5. Altering patterns of reward
Often the study of the consequences that follow problematic behaviour gives some clues about the rewards that are perpetu-ating the behaviour. A wife making sarcastic and cutting state-ments may stop a husband's criticising and complaining, and in this way she may find that her behaviour is being unwit-tingly rewarded by her husband. Altering the pattern of rewards that follow behaviour will clearly lead to change.

It is, of course, useful to study rewards so that you can see how they perpetuate behaviour. More important in a self-change programme, however, is the use of reward to encourage change. For example, where the motivation to record is lacking, a person can give him or herself a reward for conscientious recording; where antecedents are to be avoided, reward can accompany such avoidance; where there is a decrease in the frequency of problematic behaviour, again reward can follow.

There are various characteristics of the ideal reward. It should be strong in its rewarding value and easily accessible. It should not be a reward that is indispensable to a person's life, as in this case failure to gain it would produce a difficult situation and increase the temptation to give up the self-change plan.

Reward of any element of the self-change programme should be done immediately. Unfortunately this is not always possible since, amongst other things, a reward that is applied too often will lose its value. To take a simple example, if a man who wished to give up smoking rewarded himself with a chocolate every time he avoided smoking and 'smoking situations', he would, after eating half a box of chocolates, not find the prospect of yet another chocolate a rewarding one. With this kind of reward a person will quickly reach a state of satiation.

In order to overcome this difficulty, tokens or points may be used, accumulating them up to a specified number that then qualifies a person for a certain tangible reward. He or she can award points for refraining from the forbidden behaviour and these points can then be used to fulfil a range of desires – two points for a television programme, five for an evening out and so on.

Step 6. Checking changes in the frequency or duration of the problem

Clearly if rewards are effective, there will be a change in the frequency of the problematic behaviour, and this will be seen provided recording is continued throughout the self-change process.

It is not unusual to find that there are some modifications that must be made to the programme in order to make it more effective. Later we will review problems that may impair success, along with some ideas that will contribute to more effective plans.

Increasing the frequency of appropriate behaviour

Increasing the frequency of behaviour follows lines similar to those outlined above: specify the behaviour that is desirable, obtain a baseline, apply a reward for increases in frequency and look critically at the effectiveness of the programme.

Certain principles aid in the development of new behaviour and we will look at some examples of these, namely using a model and incremental change.

A person may lack a certain type of behaviour. A woman who was worried about the fact that she seemed always to behave in a submissive manner wanted to be able to express herself more assertively. In order to create the behaviour that was lacking, she first found an effective model, a person who appropriately expressed assertive behaviour. She then copied this model.

This woman also wished to have more friends and she noticed that others talked very much more than she did. Her aim was to overcome her reluctance and to talk freely to others on a range of topics, both personal and otherwise. She decided to do this in a step by step or 'incremental' fashion. She decided to reward herself for talking about 'safe' topics, such as the weather. Later, by progressive steps, she moved on to more personal and controversial topics.

Incremental progress like this is often interrupted by what are called 'plateaux'. These are periods in which no progress is made. Any person relying on a step-by-step programme is likely to remain at some levels longer than at others. This temporary delay in progress should be accepted as quite natural. Of course, a person will eventually not be able to progress further in a behaviour change plan because an appropriate level of performance has been reached.

One advantage of the incremental approach is that no matter how small each step happens to be, provided they continue to occur, they will ultimately add up to significant change. An incremental approach can also be used in an effort to reduce undesirable behaviour. Here gradual, rewarded reduction in a habit is much less demanding than a sudden stop. The easily gained successes that are achieved in the first steps towards change encourage further progress.

Combining an increase in desirable with a decrease in undesirable behaviour

An increase in desirable behaviour can be combined with a decrease in undesirable behaviour. This involves using one response to replace another. Losing one's temper can be replaced by concentrating on communicating verbally and with some precision what one is feeling. Here one response is exchanged for another that is incompatible with it. You cannot have a tantrum and talk about your anger at the same time.

What is being suggested here can follow the same kind of steps that are outlined above. Suppose, instead of becoming impulsively angry when her husband annoys her, a woman wishes to talk more freely about her frustrations. She may start by measuring how frequently she talks about her feelings to her husband. Once she has established this baseline, she may then reward herself for talking more openly and record the extent of these changes.

Changing emotional reactions

In a self-change programme thoughts and feelings can be studied in a number of ways. They may be regarded as an aspect of the situation that exercises stimulus control over behaviour. Second, they may be studied, as problematic behaviour is studied, by looking at the situations that create certain thoughts and feelings. Finally, they can often be studied not as thoughts and feelings but purely as the behaviour that expresses them, depressed feelings examined by looking at the depressed behaviour they produce, for example. We will look at these three ways of studying thoughts and feelings in turn.

Thoughts or emotional reactions can be viewed as conditions that precede behaviour, that is, as antecedents that exercise stimulus control over certain forms of behaviour. A man who reacts to each woman he meets with the thought, 'She won't like me!' behaves in a way that is too shy and tentative to be effective. The thought is the condition that precedes the behaviour. For this reason, as mentioned earlier, it is always worthwhile when recording behaviour to record associated thoughts and feelings.

Thoughts and feelings can be managed in the same way as other antecedents. The man in the last example could start his self-change programme by rewarding himself whenever he changes what he is saying to himself. He is especially likely to do this if he understands the connection between what he says and his subsequent behaviour.

An alternative to regarding thoughts and feelings as antecedents is to study thoughts and feelings as one would behaviour, looking at the conditions that precede thoughts and feelings and the consequences that follow. When this approach is adopted, you will find that there are certain conditions that always spark off specific thoughts and feelings, and that there are often rewarding consequences that follow. Some students often react to the ponderous atmosphere of the library by day-dreaming, and this in turn, although academically unproductive, is rewarded with a pleasant mood. A student who discovers the relation between a library and day-dreaming may wish, at least for a while, to change his or her place of study in order to overcome the stimulus control of the library.

If thoughts and emotional reactions are scrutinised in the same way as behaviour, they will be found to obey the same rules. Consequently the frequency of undesirable thoughts can be reduced by reward, and the frequency of desirable thoughts can be increased by reward.

Sometimes emotional reactions can be translated into forms of behaviour. Depression, for example, may involve inactivity and verbal statements that express sadness and irritability. Eliminating and replacing the behaviour that constitutes the depression can sometimes be the key to curing it. A depressed person who plans enjoyable behaviour, such as a walk in the park, talking to another about sport or watching a favourite television programme, may well find a significant lifting of his or her mood (Lewinsohn and Libet, 1972).

Thoughts, just like behaviour, can be attributed to personality

By using the word 'aggressive' not only may other people attribute this characteristic to a certain person but this person may also apply this word to him or herself. The same process may go on with regard to emotional feelings and the words used to describe these. Having feelings that a person regards as indicative of depression can lead a person to describe him or herself as depressed and ignore the set of circumstances that is regularly associated with a depressive episode.

Watson and Tharp (1977) give an interesting example of a woman who described herself as depressed. When asked to keep a record of the forms in which her depression was expressed, she found that these forms occupied such a small proportion of all her experience that she ceased to regard herself as depressed.

Difficulties that may arise with a self-change plan

Several difficulties can arise with a self-change plan. One important implication of this is that the plan will usually need to be modified as time goes by. Four types of difficulty are discussed below.

1. A lack of willpower
The first difficulty a person may face is a lack of willpower, the willpower to design and carry out a programme for changing behaviour. This is likely to be the case if he or she has failed in self-change efforts in the past.

The behaviourist, however, sees motives as activated by rewards, and a person will seek change and set up a self-change programme when steps to do so are rewarded. If we define a lack of willpower in behaviourist terms, we would say that this is an apathetic response to certain personal problems and that this response has been produced by past outcomes that have been unrewarding. In other words efforts to change have not been rewarded because they have not met with success in the past and have led to discouragement. To overcome this problem rewards should follow the planning and start of the process of change.

2. Problems with recording

Recording may involve a number of problems. Four will be mentioned here. First, a person may not find it easy to keep a strict tally and make notes about the problematic behaviour. The simplest solution to this is to systematically reward good record keeping.

Fluctuations in behaviour may occur which make it relatively difficult to obtain a baseline, the average rate of behaviour per day, within 7 days, so a longer period of 2 weeks or more may be necessary. If fluctuations do occur, further scrutiny may well reveal antecedent and consequent causes. Generally speaking recording in the baseline period should stop when there is a good understanding of the circumstances surrounding behaviour.

Many self-change programmes are given up prematurely because of a failure to collect enough information and to collect it accurately. Also many programmes are impaired because recording is abandoned too early, so that either a person underestimates progress and is discouraged from continuing, or overestimates progress and continues with an ineffective plan.

Recording before behaviour occurs has a greater effect on reducing the frequency of problematic behaviour than does recording after it has occurred. For example, those who record the number of calories before they eat actually eat less than those who record calories after they have eaten (Bellak, *et al.*, 1974). No doubt one reason for this is that there is a break in the chain of events that led to overeating; as a person stops to record there is a break between the situational cues that cause the behaviour of eating.

Where a stimulus has exercised stimulus control over behaviour for a long time, a person may find it difficult to gain conscious awareness of the link between behaviour and antecedents. A person may, for example, light and smoke a cigarette so automatically that he or she does so without being aware of it. Since conscious awareness is important for the recording and subsequent control of behaviour, it may be necessary to gain awareness by self-consciously practising the behaviour concerned. A person explicitly says to him or herself, 'Now I am taking out my cigarettes and matches. I am striking a match and lighting my cigarette...'.

3. Problems in identifying behaviour

Turning now from recording to actual behaviour, a person may find it difficult to specify the actual behaviour he or she wishes to change. The woman cited above, for example, who wished to increase her circle of friends, could go no further than saying that she did not get on with people very well. Observation of her own behaviour helped, and she identified three or four pieces of behaviour that seemed to be part of the problem. In one situation she said little, in another she contributed tentatively and reticently to a conversation, and in a third situation she said to herself, 'No-one here likes me.'

In attempting to specify behaviour she could also enlist the help of others, asking them to observe her and give her some guidance on how she could improve. Such guidance should always take a positive form, suggesting positive changes in behaviour rather than negatively criticising what she was doing wrong.

Finally, in order to identify appropriate behaviour she could (and did) observe others who were socially more successful. She learned from these models and, as suggested earlier, used them to produce new behaviour of her own.

4. Problems with antecedents

There may be too many antecedent conditions for a person to deal with. We have already seen an example of this in the man who smokes when he wakes in the morning, after breakfast, in the car going to work and so on. Once he has limited his smoking only to certain situations and not others, he can then use the two-stage process suggested above. This two-stage process is that, first, he should avoid antecedent conditions and, second, he should reintroduce himself to them gradually.

5. Problems identifying rewarding consequences

Just as identifying behaviour so that it can be changed may sometimes prove difficult, so also can identifying a reward in the consequences that follow behaviour. The simplest reason for this is that rewards do not occur sufficiently frequently to be identified.

We can exemplify the problem of an infrequent reward in the following way. Suppose a response is rewarded on average every tenth time it occurs and suppose the response occurs five times per week. A person recording in the baseline period would need 2 weeks to observe only one instance of the reward in operation. Needless to say, it would be difficult to discern a reward at such an infrequent rate.

It is important to note that finding the reward of current behaviour is much less important than being able to apply a potent reward that establishes each step towards change.

11 THE BEHAVIOURIST APPROACH TO THE PROBLEMATIC BEHAVIOUR OF CHILDREN

SUMMARY

This chapter contains two sections. The first and larger of the two deals with the problem of reducing or eliminating a child's inappropriate or undesirable behaviour. It also explains how to recognise when behaviour is truly problematic and when not, and examines the nature and effects of punishment.

The second section of this chapter deals with the promotion of behaviour that is acceptable and desirable. It begins with an explanation of a child's use of imitation and then moves on to look briefly at training children in social skills.

Introduction

The previous chapter began with an explanation of certain reservations that one may have about self-help books. Similar reservations apply to instructions given in this chapter. Having background knowledge of a specific problem before applying general principles of change and having the help of a therapist are both desirable. With regard to the latter, for example, Matson and Ollendick (1977) found that four out of five mothers following instructions aimed at overcoming problems associated with toilet training were successful when assisted by a therapist compared with only one out of five following instructions on their own. These researchers also found that negative emotional feelings arising between mother and child were much more likely in a group of mothers who did not have the aid of a therapist.

There are two main types of change that a behaviourist programme for children can accomplish. One involves the reduction or elimination of behaviour that is unacceptable or inappropriate. This would include behaviours such as temper tantrums and stealing.

A second type of behavioural change involves the learning of or an increase in acceptable and appropriate behaviour. Here a desirable form of behaviour does not occur at all or does not occur sufficiently frequently. The lack of appropriate social behaviour is one example that is examined in some detail later in this chapter.

Occasionally a third kind of change is required. A child shows a certain kind of behaviour but in the wrong circumstances, and steps must be taken to see that it is expressed in more appropriate circumstances. For example, an adolescent may be too compliant in a delinquent peer group and insufficiently compliant with members of his or her own family.

Before considering the steps that (say) a parent may take in reducing the frequency of undesirable behaviour or eliminating it altogether, there are two issues that are addressed below. The first concerns how to discern whether a problem is sufficiently serious to warrant special attention. The second concerns the limitations of using punishment to change or control behaviour.

How to decide when a difficulty is a problem

Deciding when behavioural difficulties are sufficiently serious to demand treatment is a matter of judgement. Parents are not always good at making this judgement. When parents seek help with what they regard as a problem child, it may well be that their child is no more deviant than the average child. Two criteria can be used to clarify when a difficulty should be given special attention.

1. First, problems that are seen as originating in the child's personality are often caused by circumstances. For example, a teacher may describe a child as aggressive. Further investigation may demonstrate that it is only in relation to this particular teacher that the child behaves aggressively. He or she is not like this in other relationships – with parents, peers or for that matter other teachers. When the teacher attributes the problem to the child's personality, he or she fails to recognise that it is associated with certain conditions that set off aggressive behaviour.

   A similar problem sometimes happens with parents who complain that they can no longer control their child. Again further investigation shows that this is a problem limited very much to the home and is not present in other settings, such as school. Where a problem is occurring in only one type of setting, the circumstances that are causing it must be identified so that they can be managed in some way, either eliminating them or getting the child, parent or teacher to recognise and handle them differently.

   Occasionally, but fortunately rarely, a child will be found to be behaving badly, for example aggressively or uncooperatively, in a wide range of settings – at home, at school, with his or her peers and so on. When this occurs, it more often than not denotes a problem that is so serious that it requires removal of the child from the circumstances that are perpetuating the problem. This removal must be followed by very special treatment.

2. Second, it is important to check that parents who identify a problem are not focusing on behaviour that, in our culture, is part of normal development. In this regard a number of helpful tables have been produced that show the frequency

of particular problems in different age groups for boys and for girls (see, for example, Shepherd *et al.*, 1971). This kind of table shows that food fads occur in the 5–14-year-old age group at the average rate of one in five children. Clearly food fads occur sufficiently frequently for them to be regarded as a natural event in the process of growing up. On the other hand very destructive behaviour occurs on average in less than half a per cent of girls. One could argue therefore, from its relative infrequency in this group, that when it does occur it should be given serious attention.

Incidentally it is worthwhile checking whether behaviour is judged to be odd, unusual or bad by the culture since (whether or not it *is* actually odd, unusual or bad), it will if it continues, inhibit or interfere with the child's natural processes of psychological growth. This is partly because those close to the child treat him or her differently from other children and as a result the child is disadvantaged or even psychologically damaged.

Punishment as a means of control

Often a parent will use punishment to eliminate a child's undesirable behaviour. This is generally a poor and inefficient means of training since the child is learning what is wrong but not what is right. The child can only guess at what is the right or appropriate behaviour. This is particularly true if the child is punished without explanation and the punishment is administered inconsistently, depending on whatever mood the parent happens to be in.

Punishment is also a poor training device because it can arouse in the punished child high levels of resentment, fear and anxiety. Little or no learning takes place in conditions of high emotional arousal because the child focuses on coping with the arousal rather than on what the parent is attempting to instil. Not only are high levels of arousal distracting but they also make it difficult to think clearly and learn.

The unpleasant experience of being punished can become associated with the person who is doing the punishing. This can have a bad effect on the relationship between parent and child, especially if the only interaction between parent and child involves punishment. A situation that exemplifies this well is one in which children are left to do what they wish until they do something wrong and then they are punished for it. Punishment then becomes the major or only grounds for contact between a parent and child. Particularly if parents are busy with other things, they can look back over several hours and discover that the only times they had anything to do with their children was when their children did something wrong and were chastised for it. If a significant proportion of a parent's interaction with a child is on the grounds of irritation, annoyance and punishment, their relationship will not be a good one.

A technique more effective than punishing wrong behaviour is the reward of what is desirable or appropriate. Through this the child learns exactly what is required and the good feelings associated with reward also become associated with the relationship the child has with the parent. Some behaviourists have suggested that parents 'catch their child doing something good' in order to confirm and increase the frequency of acceptable behaviour. If they do this, they will also develop a reciprocal process with their child: as the parents provide rewards, the child produces behaviour that the parents find rewarding, and the parents in turn are more rewarding to the child.

Some writers have argued for a limited role for punishment in childrearing. Jehu (1966), for example, describes the problems associated with a child who is impulsively running off the pavement into the road. Rewarding such a child for staying on the pavement will ultimately be effective but the child's learning in response to reward may be too slow to prevent an accident. While rewarding the child for staying on the pavement, the parent may then consider punishing the child whenever he or she runs off the pavement since this will temporarily lower the frequency of this dangerous behaviour.

One of the reasons for the popularity of punishment in spite of it being an inefficient method of training is that it can be rewarding for the person giving it. The feelings of anger and upset following a child's bad behaviour can be relieved by physically punishing the child. Such relief acts as a reward. Although this is a dubious basis for administering punishment, it is infinitely preferable to a situation in which a parent refrains from physically chastising a child but emotionally hounds the child for days or weeks because of continuing feelings of resentment over what the child has done.

Punishment may be rewarding not only for a parent but also, perversely, for a child. In the normal course of events children would prefer positive responses, such as affection, care, concern and so on, from parents. If parents do not provide these, the next most preferred response is one of punishment and rejection. At least by provoking this response the child has exerted some influence over his or her situation. Such influence is valued more highly than indifference, the worst kind of treatment a child can receive. For children who have been treated indifferently by their families, rejection and punishment can paradoxically become rewards.

Decreasing the frequency of unacceptable behaviour: steps necessary for change

Let us suppose that a father and mother approached the school psychological service for help in dealing with the problematic behaviour of their child. They might be asked by an educational psychologist to use the following steps to bring about change.

1. *Find out what the problematic behaviour is. What does the child say or do?*
Parents often describe their child's problems in terms of personality traits – he or she is aggressive, impulsive, uncooperative and so on. Because they take this view they often find it difficult to specify what the child is doing wrong in purely

behavioural terms. They must learn to ask themselves, 'What precisely does the child say or do?'

There is another difficulty that arises when a child's problem is seen as having its origins in personality traits. Once a negative characteristic is attributed to the child – that perhaps he or she is regarded as disobedient – the rest of the personality is assumed to be bad. In other words a parent who constantly thinks of those instances in which a child was disobedient and uncooperative may soon end up feeling that the 'whole of' their child is essentially bad.

The development of negative feelings in this way can then affect all future judgements of the child. When, on occasion, the child does behave obediently or cooperatively, the parents interpret this behaviour in the light of the bad feelings they already have of the child. They do not accept good behaviour at face value and, when it occurs, are inclined to ask, 'Why is my child behaving like this? Is this an attempt to get round me?'

It is also possible that bad feelings that have their origins in situations that have nothing to do with a child may affect the way in which his or her behaviour is regarded. Research has shown, for example, that the more stress there is in a marriage relationship, the more negatively a child's bad behaviour will be regarded, and that any improvements in the marriage result in less negativity towards the child (Rabin, 1981). An unhappy marriage relationship may result in parents unjustifiably seeking help for what they regard as their child's problematic behaviour.

In order to offset these tendencies and improve communication with the child, the parents can be encouraged to think and talk in terms not of personality traits but in terms only of behaviour. Thus, instead of describing a child as 'lazy', parents should specify behaviour, pointing out that their child has (say) failed to keep his or her room tidy. Specifying behaviour is a direct and clear way of communicating with the child and implies, 'You have behaved like this but you could have behaved otherwise.' This implication contrasts with using a word such as 'lazy', which implies, 'You need to change your personality', which, as has been suggested elsewhere in this book, is a difficult if not impossible thing to do.

2. Find out what leads up to and what follows the problematic behaviour

As we have seen when considering whether behaviour should be defined as problematic, a problem is sometimes attributed to the child's personality when it should be attributed to the situation that generates the behaviour. In order to understand the link between situation and behaviour, what precedes and what follows behaviour should be noted. This involves studying the so-called 'antecedents' and 'consequences'.

Parents often take the view that behaviour 'just happens'. However, if the problematic behaviour sometimes occurs and sometimes does not, a behaviourist will look for a pattern that underlies its disappearance and its reappearance. The rationale for looking for a pattern is that, when the behaviour occurs, some principle is operating to make it occur. When it is not occurring some principle is at work to prevent it occurring. Hence studying antecedents can lead to an understanding of what causes and what ameliorates problematic behaviour.

What precedes behaviour can be recorded in terms of time (when it happened), place (where it happened) and circumstances (what was happening). It may be, for example, that a child has tantrums only at meals and before bedtime, and only with one of his or her parents and not the other.

Identifying consequences means looking at the change that has been brought about in a situation by the behaviour. Often behaving badly brings about beneficial changes for the child. Just how the child is rewarded should be noted, along with the possible reasons for the reward.

Sometimes it is difficult to identify a reward. One important reason for this is that the child's behaviour has been rewarded infrequently and irregularly. Paradoxically this pattern of reward leads to establishing a greater persistence in behaviour than frequent and regular reward, as the following example shows.

A psychologist was asked to see a 4-year-old child who had temper tantrums lasting up to 3 hours. Her investigations showed that the child's mother inconsistently and irregularly rewarded the child's demanding behaviour. Unknowingly this mother was training her young boy to persist in his tantrums until he got what he wanted. For example, after the child had watched several television programmes he would demand to see yet another. If his mother refused to let him do this, he would have a tantrum. After 2 or 3 minutes his mother gave in to his demand and allowed him to watch some more television. But she told him that at the end of the next programme she would not let him watch another. When this next programme ended he made another request to continue watching and when his mother refused he had another tantrum. At first she stuck to her guns and refused to give in, but after about 6 minutes she relented and let him watch another programme. Again she vowed she would not on future occasions relent but found herself unable to resist when he had been shouting, angry and upset for 15 minutes, at which point she again let him have his way. This pattern tended to be repeated day after day until the boy was capable of continuing his tantrums for hours. Although rewards came very infrequently, they nevertheless established a very persistent pattern of behaviour.

3. List the child's assets and assemble a credit/debit list

Just as parents may be unable specifically to identify undesirable behaviour (dwelling on what they see as problems in the child's personality and using words such as 'aggressive' and 'uncooperative'), they may in the same way be unable to identify the child's positive behaviours or assets. This is because, as suggested earlier, they judge the child's behaviour in the light of already well-established negative feelings about him or her. They may need help to recognise and acknowledge positive forms of the child's behaviour.

Listing the child's assets will help in 'catching him or her in doing something good'. Behaviourists argue that, if good behaviour is rewarded, it will increase in frequency or duration. As a result the child spends more time 'being good', leaving less time available for problematic behaviour.

Becoming aware of the child's assets will also give the parents some encouragement if they regard themselves as having failed as parents. They may discover that there is much that their child does that is reasonable or good. They may also discover that they are focusing on a relatively isolated feature of their child's life. They have become so totally preoccupied with this that they do not realise that it occurs very infrequently compared with the rest of the child's behaviour.

4. Identify problematic behaviours to be dealt with and then determine priorities

If the child manifests a range of problems – which is often the case – decisions about those that should be tackled first must be made. Anyone encouraging parents to use a behavioural approach will wish to achieve as early a success as possible. This success is likely to be achieved with less pressing problems. Therefore a balance must be achieved between tackling those problems that are most disturbing and those which yield relatively quickly to change.

The matter of early success is particularly important when dealing with parents who have, in the past, made several attempts at changing their child's behaviour and have failed. In behaviourist terms their past efforts have not been rewarded, and they may well be inclined to put little effort into any further attempts to produce a solution. They may even believe that a successful outcome is impossible. An early success will transform this situation.

5. Record the frequency or duration of the problematic behaviour

The previous steps establish the grounds for understanding precisely the change in behaviour that is required. The frequency or duration of the behaviour must now be recorded. This can be done in conjunction with observing and recording antecedents and consequences.

As suggested earlier parents have a general tendency to see problems in terms of personality traits and characteristics. As a result some parents may not be very good at thinking in terms of behaviour and observing it. Since recording depends on the accuracy of observations, it is important to check that parents can do this.

Since children can be adept at exploiting any inconsistencies between one parent and another, training parents in the observation of behaviour has the added advantage that they can agree precisely on which behaviours are going to be rewarded and which unacceptable behaviours need attention. This makes for clarity of communication between the parents and consistency in their responses to their child. Behaviourists regard such consistency as critical to the success of behaviour change.

The easiest method of recording is counting behavioural responses (as opposed to measuring the duration or intensity of a response). If a simple counting procedure is adopted, the parents can be provided with a tally sheet.

The process of observing and counting behaviour can in itself produce significant decreases in the problematic behaviour. Some authors (Herbert, 1981) report improvement in some 20 per cent of cases from recording alone. No doubt one of the reasons for this is that a child who knows that behaviour is being recorded also becomes an observer of his or her own behaviour and hence better able to control it.

From what is recorded the average frequency or duration of problematic behaviour for each day can be determined. This is known as the baseline. This baseline can at a later date be compared with engineered changes in the frequency of behaviour.

6. *Choose and apply a reward*

If we are to decrease the frequency of behaviour that is unacceptable or inappropriate, we can either reward demonstrable decreases or, better still, reward behaviour that is incompatible with the problematic behaviour. Talking about feelings of frustration, for example, is incompatible with actually having a temper tantrum, and it is this talking that should be rewarded.

In choosing a reward account must be taken of what specific rewards are effective with a particular child. With young, inarticulate children it may be necessary to assess the meaning of a reward by looking at what his or her behaviour is responsive to.

Concrete rewards such as sweets have a number of disadvantages. For example, they lose their capacity to reward as they are given again and again. An alternative is to use tokens as rewards. Each token is immediately given in response to appropriate behaviour. Once a number of these tokens have accumulated they can be exchanged for something that the child desires.

One of the advantages of the use of tokens is that the child's progress can be made explicit, perhaps by rewarding him or her with a 'star' that acts as a token. The obvious accumulation of stars on a chart displayed on a wall encourages further progress and no doubt increases the kind of control mentioned above that can be brought about by recording alone.

Rules for the application of a reward should be simple and applied consistently. The parents and the child should understand who does what and under which conditions.

Having selected one or two target problems, goals should be short term, and initially every effort, even those that fall short of perfection, should be rewarded. In the early stages reward should be given frequently and for closer and closer approximations of the target behaviour. In the later stages reward should be given less frequently as this will make the improved behaviour more persistent.

Increasing the frequency of acceptable behaviour: models and the development of behaviour

Children (and adults) generally do not create entirely new behaviour but imitate the modelled behaviour of those they have observed. The importance of models can be demonstrated in the following way.

Imagine I am an infant and that, for the first time in my life, I am frustrated and this is resulting in feelings of anger and rage. This anger or rage exists as an urge or impulse or pressure inside me that seeks expression. If I don't know how to transform what is going on inside me into the kind of behaviour usually associated with anger, I may show my feelings in a relatively expressionless way – I may throw myself on the floor, arms flailing and legs kicking in a temper tantrum.

The alternative to resorting to this kind of behaviour (not that a child *consciously* does this) is to look round my family and ask, 'How do members of my family behave when they feel angry?' or, more specifically, 'How does my father or mother behave when angry?' Asking these questions leads to the identification of a model that can be imitated or copied and who will enable me to translate my angry feelings into behaviour.

Bandura (1977) and his colleagues have made a number of experimental investigations of imitative behaviour. In one of these Bandura tested the hypothesis that children exposed to an aggressive adult model will, when made to feel angry themselves, copy the adult model. He first gave children an opportunity to watch an adult maltreating a doll, kicking, punching and hammering it with a mallet. Following this he attempted to rouse the children's anger by initially giving them attractive toys to play with and then removing the toys, explaining that these toys were to be reserved for other children. After their removal the children were given less attractive toys, amongst which were cars and crayons, which could be used in a non-aggressive manner, and the doll that had been attacked by the adult.

Bandura found that once their aggressive feelings were aroused, the children chose the doll and attacked it. Not only this but they attacked it in ways that were clearly imitative of the adult they had observed earlier. In order to establish the validity of what he found, Bandura carried out a similar procedure with a second group of children. This group was subjected to the same experiences as the first except that they were not given the opportunity to observe the adult model. The behaviour that these children exhibited when their anger was aroused was in no way like that of the original group of children.

Not only does observation of a model produce learned behaviour but so also does perception of the consequences of the model's behaviour. Hartrup (1974), for example, conducted an experiment similar to that of Bandura. An aggressive model was seen by one group of children to be rewarded for his behaviour, by another to be punished and by a third to be sometimes punished and sometimes rewarded. The observation of rewarded and/or punished behaviour had clear effects on the children; the first group were seen to be most aggressive, the second group showed no imitative behaviour and the third group showed a moderate level of aggression. Clearly the freedom with which the children expressed their aggression was influenced by the model and the observed consequences of the model's behaviour.

For behaviourists like Bandura the effect of a model has become a major focus of interest. Copying a model is a much more efficient method of learning than is producing responses that are followed by reward. Learning to swim or drive a car by the reinforcement of each appropriate action is a slow if not hazardous process. The would-be swimmer or driver would have to select, create and carry out each action and would have to cope with the heightened emotion of the desire for success and the fear of failure. Those who observe a competent model, on the other hand, can give their undivided attention to learning the correct pattern of behaviour.

The actions of a model can therefore provide a useful and efficient training device for forms of appropriate behaviour that a child may lack. Of special interest are those forms that are necessary for socially skilled performances (Cartledge and Milburn, 1980).

Social skills

Socially skilled children (or adults) are those who can bring their influence to bear in their relationships in a manner that is appropriate or acceptable. This influence is often used to satisfy certain needs, such as those for love and attention. In contrast socially unskilled children (and adults) either cannot bring their influence to bear or do so in a manner that is inappropriate. A child, for example, may be incapable of satisfying his or her need for attention or does satisfy it but in a manner that is unacceptable.

For a child, developing a skill depends on a number of factors. Let us take the skill of engaging another child in conversation. We might start by getting a child to practise asking three types of question: first a general question, 'Do you live near here?' or 'Is the school you go to a big school with lots of children or fairly small?', then a more detailed question, 'How long does it take you to get from home to your school?' or 'What time does your school finish in the afternoon?', and finally a question that brings feelings to the surface, 'What is your favourite lesson?' or 'Do you think the school you go to is a good one?'

For this skill to develop the child must have certain mental and emotional capacities. As these capacities develop with increasing age, it is important to be able to recognise what a child of a particular age is capable of. Assuming the child has the capacity and ability, he or she must have the component skills and must be able to synthesise these into a composite set of actions. A model can demonstrate how skills are synthesised or integrated.

Sometimes component skills are missing. Making it possible for a child to observe a good model helps the child to copy, create and practice forms of behaviour that are absent from his or her repertoire. The model's behaviour can be recorded on videotape and the most important aspects of the model's performance can then be pointed out to the child. Also the model's thoughts can be dubbed onto the tape so that the observer can not only mimic what is seen but also repeat the internal dialogue the model is having. This internal dialogue can contribute to the development of appropriate emotional responses. It can also aid retention and rehearsal since a model has more influence if a child can represent modelled activities using words and images than if the child relies on merely passive observation. Sometimes children can be prompted to analyse what is being observed for themselves. This is again likely to be more effective than is simply describing or explaining to the child what is taking place.

Using a model as an aid to training should be done bearing certain principles in mind. The model should be a person with whom the child can identify and, perhaps, a person with some prestige. He or she could be another child of the same age who is clearly popular. The model should be shown to be successful so that the observer expects success if he or she adopts the same behaviour. The anticipation of such success can be a strong motivating force.

A perfect standard of performance should not, however, be a requirement. Progressively better approximations to a reasonable standard should be the aim and each step towards this should be rewarded.

12 THE EXPERIMENTAL FOUNDATIONS OF BEHAVIOURISM

SUMMARY

The experimental traditions of behaviourism are based on the work of a number of investigators. Two of these, Pavlov (1850–1936) and Skinner (1904–1990), have been particularly important. In addition to their work we will look at the importance of control, a phenomenon first investigated by Seligman.

The fundamentals of behaviourism will be examined by looking at experiments that have been done on animals and drawing parallels between these and certain aspects of human behaviour.

Introduction

As mentioned in the introduction to behaviourism at the beginning of this section, early behaviourists sought to establish psychology as a scientific discipline. They did this by limiting themselves to the study of behaviour alone since this was the only aspect of a person's psychology that could be scientifically observed. They also used the experimental method to examine two of their most central interests, learning and reward. Again, as mentioned earlier, behaviourists turned initially not to human beings as experimental subjects but to simpler animals such as rats.

Pavlov's experimental work

Pavlov used dogs as experimental subjects and demonstrated a simple form of learning in which one thing is associated with another. Under conditions that were highly controlled, he rang a bell immediately before feeding a dog. By collecting the dog's saliva Pavlov showed that he learned to salivate to the ringing bell; that is, the dog had associated the bell with the presentation of food.

The experimental conditions for this kind of learning are as follows. In order to control motivation Pavlov starved his dogs to a certain percentage of their normal body weight. He placed each dog in a large box, restrained him in a harness and observed him through a one-way glass screen. Following the ringing of a bell, food was given to the dog in the form of meat powder blown into his mouth. When the interval between ringing the bell and the presentation of food was half a second, the association between the two was learned quickly and efficiently. When the interval was more or less than this, learning by association either occurred slowly or not at all.

The pattern of events that Pavlov investigated is now known as 'classical conditioning'. The word 'conditioning' essentially means 'learning' and has been used ever since Pavlov's work was translated into English and the Russian word for learning was mistranslated as 'conditioning'.

Classical conditioning occurs in the human sphere. For example, the origins of a phobia may be regarded as a simple form of associative learning. A phobia involves connecting acute anxiety with some aspect of the conditions in which the anxiety first occurs. For example, an engineer who was working in a newly painted factory suddenly discovered that his shirt sleeve was being drawn into a machine. For a few brief seconds this induced a very high level of anxiety or panic. This anxiety or panic became associated with the smell of paint so that, without understanding why, on later occasions when he could smell paint, he felt acutely fearful – he had developed a phobia for the smell of paint.

Learned discriminations

Using the experimental situation he designed, Pavlov could develop the discriminatory powers of his dogs. He could, for example, feed a dog only when he sounded a bell of a certain pitch or note; if he sounded other bells having different notes but did not follow these with the reward of food, he could train a dog to salivate to the sound of one note only. In principle this experiment can be repeated with other animals and humans to see how far reward can develop their ability to discriminate.

In response to appropriate rewards much of learning in childhood and adult life depends on the development of discrimination. A child may use the word 'cat' initially to refer to all four-legged animals. This demonstrates the process of generalisation, which is the opposite of discrimination. At a later stage a child may not only recognise the difference between a cat and other animals but will also make distinctions between one type of cat and another.

Pavlov could use his experimental situation to find out how discriminating dogs could be. In one of his investigations he shone a circle on the side of the dog's cage and followed it with food. He then shone an ellipse on the side of the cage and followed it by a punishment, a mild electric shock. He then made the circle more like an ellipse and the ellipse more like a circle to see how discriminating the dog could be. At a certain point the dog could no longer discern the difference between one shape and another and therefore did not know what to expect. This produced an unfortunate and unexpected result; the dog began to show serious signs of emotional and behavioural disturbance.

Although this experiment is in itself disturbing, it does demonstrate the general principle that emotional and behavioural problems can be produced by inappropriate experiences. In short Pavlov in this experiment had treated a dog as no dog is designed to be treated, and the result was what might be described as 'a mental breakdown'. The same principle holds good for human beings who can be similarly affected by prolonged inhumane treatment.

Extroverts, introverts and conditioning

The ease with which a person can form the simple, involuntary associations that Pavlov demonstrated can be measured. This can be done by getting a person to listen to a sound made in a pair of headphones. This sound is then immediately followed by a short blast of air onto the eye, inducing a blink. The number of pairings of noise and air blast that are necessary before a person blinks to the sound alone is a measure of their conditionability.

Eysenck (1970, 1984, 1987) reported a difference in the degree to which extroverts and introverts can be conditioned. An extrovert is a person who is outgoing and impulsive, needs to be in constant contact with people, looks for excitement and adventure, and is generally easy going. The extrovert conditions poorly if at all.

The introvert is a person who is quiet and introspective, keeps feelings and impulses under a tight rein, prefers books to people, finds excitement difficult to cope with and generally lives a well-ordered life. The introvert conditions readily, indeed perhaps too readily.

Extroversion and introversion represent different poles of what is in fact a continuum. Most people will come somewhere between these extremes. Differences of conditionability will be most marked with extreme extroverts and extreme introverts. These people will exhibit significant differences in their respective psychologies.

Because he or she conditions poorly, the extreme extrovert will not make strong associations between moral values and behaviour. Thus, particularly if they are emotionally unstable, extroverts are likely to be found much more often amongst those who are delinquent; they are, in the language of social science, 'over-represented in the delinquent population'. Not only are there likely to be moral or ethical weaknesses in the case of extroverts but they also have a tendency when things go wrong to experience the fault as lying in others rather than in themselves. This often makes them difficult to deal with.

Because he or she conditions too easily, the extreme introvert will make associations between moral values and behaviour that are too strong; if emotionally unstable, introverts are likely to be troubled, disturbed and, perhaps, disabled by unnecessarily high levels of guilt and anxiety over relatively minor moral or ethical misdemeanours. Introverts, by contrast with extroverts, are likely to blame themselves when anything goes wrong. This again can contribute to their inflated sense of guilt and anxiety.

Although introverts are less likely to be present in the delinquent population, their tendency to make associations easily can sometimes get them into trouble. Suppose, for example, that a man who has the personality of an introvert is looking from the flat in which he lives across to a neighbouring block where he sees a woman undressing. As a result of this he feels sexually stimulated. Naturally he may associate this sensation with the fact that he is seeing parts of an attractive woman's body. However, there are other associations he may make. He may associate his sensations with pieces of the woman's underwear and finds that he can reinstate pleasurable sexual feelings whenever he sees or collects such underwear in the future. Alternatively he may associate his excitement with the act of looking; that is, he becomes sexually excited by looking where he ought not.

Eysenck (1967) has explained the differences between extroverts and introverts in terms of differences of brain function. The outer covering of the brain or cortex is largely responsible for intellectual functioning. It is that part of your brain that is responsible for making sense and drawing conclusions from the marks on the pages of this book that you are reading. The cortex has two processes at work within it, excitation and inhibition. These two are in balance but the balance in extroverts and introverts is different. In extroverts the level of inhibition is high so they seek stimulation from outside. Many of the characteristics of extroverts can be regarded as a craving for the stimulation that is in short supply within the nervous system. In introverts the balance is towards excitation. The introvert has such an active cortical nervous system that it can entertain him or her in the absence of outside stimulation. In fact the cortex is so active that even a minor amount of external stimulation is experienced as unpleasant.

Amongst many pieces of evidence for these ideas on brain functioning, there is one that illustrates the difference of balance in excitation and inhibition between extroverts and introverts rather neatly. Extroverts have high pain thresholds. If you stick a pin into an extrovert, he or she may feel relatively little pain and may well regard this as a stimulating and enjoyable experience and ask you to do it again. Introverts have low pain thresholds. Just touching an introvert with a pin adds to all the stimulation that is going on in the nervous system and for that reason it is experienced as painful. Incidentally one implication of this difference in pain thresholds is that an introvert should always avoid getting into a fight with an extrovert.

What is experienced as a punishment is likely to be very different for extroverts and introverts. Extroverts may not be troubled by physical punishment but will find solitary confinement intolerable. Introverts may have no difficulty with solitary confinement will suffer badly if they are physically punished.

Conditioning and general differences in personality

According to behaviourists, if we look at why a person values something, it is because of its association with those things that fulfil more fundamental needs. Thus people value affection, money, achievement and power because at some stage these have been associated with things such as food and drink.

Pavlov demonstrated this process in the following way. When the ringing of the bell is associated with food, the bell starts to have rewarding properties of its own. Consequently once a dog has learned to salivate to the bell, a second learning experiment can be performed which demonstrates that the bell can be used as a reward.

In this second experiment, without the reward of food, the stimulus of a black square may be presented to the dog followed by the ringing of the bell. Just as the bell had been associated with food, now a black square is being associated with the bell. After several pairings of the black square and the bell, the dog will be found to be salivating to the black square when the black square is presented on its own. This proves that the bell has some capacity to reward salivating to the black square. (Of course, since the pairing of black square and bell is taking place in the absence of food, the amount of salivation to the bell is gradually being reduced because salivating to the bell is no longer being rewarded.)

Food and drink, which satisfy basic biological needs, are called primary rewards. Rewards such as the bell, or affection, money, achievement and power, are called secondary rewards.

Skinner's experimental work

Skinner constructed a cage which was fitted with a lever and a trough (Figure 12.1). When the lever was pressed, food or water could be delivered to the trough. This type of cage is known as a Skinner box, and the most frequently used experimental animals have been rats and pigeons.

A hungry rat placed in a Skinner box will sooner or later learn to press the lever for a pellet of food. This kind of learning is called 'operant learning' because the rat 'operates' on its environment in order to receive a reward. Much human learning, behaviourists believe, is brought about by behaviour 'operating' on the environment in ways that produce rewards. In contrast to the type of learning described by Pavlov, in which the animal has no control over what happens to it, the type of learning described by Skinner is called 'operant conditioning'.

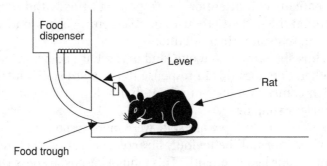

Figure 12.1 A Skinner Box

The experimental situation designed by Skinner can be used to illustrate differing ways in which operant rewards function. Here are four.

1. Behaviour shaping
A hungry rat placed in a Skinner box for the first time will, as you would expect, take some time to discover that pressing the lever results in the appearance of a food pellet in the trough. Instead of waiting for this accidental event to occur, the rat's learning can be hastened by using a process known as behaviour shaping. In this we reward the rat with a food pellet at first for moving into the half of the cage in which the lever is situated. When the rat has learned to do this, it is then rewarded

for touching the wall out of which the lever protrudes. In this way we are progressively increasing the chances of the rat pressing the lever. Much of animal training is based on the principle of behaviour shaping.

Behaviour shaping in humans, like that in animals, involves progressive changes in behaviour that follow the presentation of rewards. Consider an example. A patient, newly admitted to the ward of a mental hospital, at first receives attention for the mildly eccentric behaviour that she exhibits. Then as the staff become accustomed to this behaviour, they no longer reward the patient with attention. In response to this withdrawal of attention the patient produces more eccentric behaviour. This, in turn, reinstates their attention.

Thus she moves from one kind or level of odd behaviour to another. She does this in response to the ward staff's interest, which comes and goes in a way that follows the principle of behaviour shaping.

If, incidentally, the ward staff were more responsive to 'ordinary' or 'normal' behaviour, bizarre or eccentric behaviour would occur less frequently. This kind of responsiveness would also be more humane.

2.   The disappearance of behaviour or extinction

If, after learning to press the lever of a Skinner box for the reward of a food pellet, a rat is no longer rewarded, the rat will, as common sense predicts, eventually give up pressing the lever. By withdrawing reward the lever-pressing behaviour is 'extinguished'.

We can regard certain forms of depression as a human parallel to the extinction process. When, as happens for the rat, a source of reward is removed, the behaviour that is perpetuated by that reward will cease.

Let us take an example from bereavement, in which depression is a frequent occurrence. A man who has a good relationship with his wife will have a wide range of his behaviours rewarded by her. Just as the lever-pressing behaviour of the rat depends on the delivery of food, so a great deal of this man's behaviour depends on the rewards his spouse provides. When she dies, of course, she will no longer provide these rewards, and, correspondingly, a lot of his behaviour will be extinguished. He may well be described as being apathetic and depressed, although a more accurate description would be that he has ceased behaving. With the discovery of fresh sources of reward, his behaviour may be regarded as having started up again.

3. Infrequent reward or partial reinforcement

A rat may be rewarded not for each time it presses the lever but for every fourth time it presses the lever. Rewarding each response is referred to as a 'continuous reinforcement schedule' whereas rewarding every fourth response is referred to as a 'partial reinforcement schedule'. Behaviourists generally prefer the term 'reinforcement' to 'reward', even though the two words are essentially synonymous.

There are several types of partial reinforcement schedule, each developing their own characteristic rates of work. Being rewarded for every fourth response, equivalent to piece work, is called a 'fixed ratio schedule'. Another type of schedule is the 'fixed interval schedule' in which there is a time gap of perhaps 2 minutes between one rewarded response and another. There are also 'variable ratio schedules' and 'variable interval schedules' in which the number of responses or the time interval required for reward varies randomly. Rewards gained from gambling usually follow a variable schedule.

The important characteristic of partial reinforcement schedules is that they make behaviour much more persistent. This can be demonstrated in the following way. Suppose a hungry rat is taught to press the lever of a Skinner box in order to receive food. To make sure the animal has learned to press the lever, we reward it 100 times. We then cease rewarding the rat and count the number of responses it makes before lever pressing is extinguished. Usually, depending on how hungry the rat is, this will amount to around 100 (unrewarded) responses.

Suppose we take a second rat but this time we reward it not for each lever press but for every fourth lever press. Again we reward it 100 times and then we cease rewarding it. The number of responses this second rat makes before lever pressing is extinguished will come to around 175. In other words this second rat is much more persistent than the first.

We can draw a human parallel with the different behaviour of these two rats. We can compare our first rat with spoilt children who, as a matter of course, are rewarded for every response. Psychologists know that these children cannot tolerate frustration and will not persist in the face of difficulty.

The rat who is rewarded for every fourth response is rather like those children who constantly pester or nag. They learn to persist because their parents, by eventually giving in, have trained them to make a number of responses before they gain their reward.

Partial reinforcement may be combined with behaviour shaping. In the case of the eccentric, mentally disordered patient described above, the staff may inadvertently provide rewards on a partial reinforcement schedule. They reward occasionally and infrequently and contribute to the persistence of the patient's behaviour.

You may surmise that a possible solution to the problems caused by partial reinforcement would involve not giving in to undesirable behaviour and leaving it permanently unrewarded by ignoring it. Extinguishing behaviour by ignoring it is not, however, always easy. When a rat that has become accustomed to being rewarded for lever pressing no longer receives food, that rat will often show a burst of very frequent and persistent activity. The same also proves true in human beings. A child who has regularly but infrequently gained the reward of attention for bad behaviour will initially become much more persistent when this bad behaviour is first ignored. This persistence often proves to be a storm too strong for the parents to weather.

4. Punishment

Before leaving what we might describe as the working principles of reward, we will look briefly at the nature of punishment. Punishment is often regarded as the opposite of reward. As will become clear punishment is much more complex.

Let us look at an experiment that compares punished with unpunished rats. Two groups of rats were trained to press the lever of a Skinner box to obtain food. The responses of the first group were extinguished in the normal way by not reinforcing lever presses. The responses of the second group were also extinguished, but for the first 5 minutes of the extinction procedure they were punished by being given a mild electric shock through the lever.

As you might expect the effect of the punishment was to accelerate the extinction process. In comparison with the first, nonshocked group, the shocked group markedly (and immediately) lowered their response rate. Surprisingly, however, at the end of the 5-minute period, when the punishment ceased, the second group started to make more responses than the first (Figure 12.2). The result of this was that the number of responses to extinction was ultimately the same for both groups.

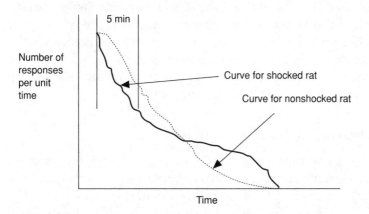

Figure 12.2 The extinction process for a punished and unpunished rat

In the light of this finding we might say that when a rat has been regularly rewarded for pressing a lever, it builds up a stock of responses that it releases in the extinction process. There is a technical term for this stock of responses. It is called a 'reflex reserve'. Once this reflex reserve has formed, it is unaffected by mild punishment.

This is not to say that mild punishment has no effect at all. Clearly it temporarily lowers the response rate. As one would expect, severe punishment enhances this effect, drastically reducing the rate, perhaps eliminating lever pressing altogether. In this case, however, the rat will show signs of gross disturbance. It will tremble, be excited and may urinate and defecate frequently and apparently involuntarily.

We can draw some important conclusions from this experiment. Unless punishment is severe, the behaviour it is meant to suppress will reappear. If it *is* severe it generates disturbing levels of fear and anxiety.

As suggested in the previous chapter, a child (or adult) will not learn best while experiencing the emotional consequences of punishment. If punishment is severe (and therefore effective) a great deal of resentment will be felt towards the person doing it. This resentment can be described and analysed in terms of the associative form of learning that Pavlov investigated. When one person punishes another, the presence or 'stimulus' of that person will become associated with the unpleasant effects of punishment, effects such as fear and anxiety. Needless to say this is not good for the relationship between the punisher and the punished.

Seligman's work and the nature of rewards

Why is a reward rewarding? If we think of 'operant' rewards, there are two important answers that behaviourists can give to this question. First, a reward maintains or increases the frequency of a pattern of behaviour because it satisfies a need. Second, and perhaps more fundamentally, a reward gives evidence to people of the control they have over their environment. It is this matter of control that we will look at in detail.

The importance of control has come to light only relatively recently, mainly through the work of Martin Seligman (1975; Mikulincer, 1994), who looked at what happened to animals and people who were deprived of the control they were normally able to exercise over their environment. Let us look at two animal experiments and two experiments with human beings that illustrate the principles that Seligman unearthed.

His interest in control developed in the following way. He was repeating some work that had been done a number of years previously that had shown how dogs can learn to escape from an unpleasant situation. We will digress for a moment to describe this work.

Learned avoidance

The learning of escape behaviour can be demonstrated in the following way. A dog is placed in what is known as a shuttle box (Figure 12.3). This is a box divided in the middle by a low wall. On one side of the wall the floor is made of a steel grill. Once the dog is placed in the box a buzzer is sounded, and 10 seconds later the dog receives a continuous, mild electric shock through the steel grill.

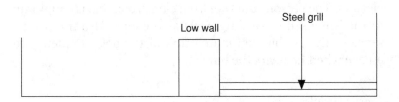

Figure 12.3 Shuttle box

Not surprisingly, when the shock begins, the dog will yelp and jump around. Sooner or later he will escape by jumping over the wall. After one or two more experiences of buzzer followed by shock, the dog will successfully escape all future shocks, jumping over the wall in response to the buzzer. This avoidance of the shock is very persistent. The dog will respond to several thousand soundings of the buzzer without any sign of its escape response decaying.

Let us look for a moment at the parallels between what we know of the dog's behaviour and the nature of a phobia. Once the dog has learned that the buzzer is followed by shock, the buzzer induces a state of fear, and this fear can be brought to an end by escape. The termination of the fear and anxiety acts as a reward and as a consequence the dog is caught up in a self-rewarding cycle.

BUZZER (followed 10 seconds later by) **SHOCK**

(induces) **FEAR**

ESCAPE (from fear is) **REWARDING**

In the case of a phobia, claustrophobia for example, the stimulus of a confined space such as an elevator acts in the same way as the buzzer. It induces a sense of fear and anxiety. This fear and anxiety can be terminated by avoiding the elevator. The person suffering from claustrophobia is caught up in the same self-rewarding cycle as the dog. Also the persistence of the phobia will match that of the dog's tendency to escape when he hears the buzzer.

Learned helplessness

Seligman was interested in the effects of giving a dog some experience of shock before entering the shuttle box. Once this had been given to a dog, he was then placed in the box, the buzzer was sounded and 10 seconds later the shock was turned on. Initially this dog behaved in the expected way, running and jumping around. However, his behaviour dramatically changed after about 30 seconds, with the dog lying down on the grill and whining. Further experiences in the shuttle box led to the dog showing less of a tendency to struggle and more of a passive acceptance of his fate.

By giving the dog an unpleasant experience over which it had no control before entering the box, Seligman had produced a condition that he called 'learned helplessness'. This condition was surprisingly difficult to overcome.

With those dogs in whom he had produced a state of helplessness, Seligman tried a variety of methods to overcome the problem. He tried lowering the height of the wall in the shuttle box, removing the wall altogether, placing food in the other side of the box and putting a harness on the dog and dragging him across the wall. In this last case – and this demonstrates the persistence of the problem – Seligman had to drag each dog over the wall at least 24 times, and with some dogs over 200 times, before the animal started to show signs of overcoming his helplessness.

To describe a second animal experiment, Richter (cited in Seligman, 1975) found that a wild rat will swim in a tank of water at body temperature for about 60 hours before giving up so that it must be rescued. In contrast he found that a wild rat that has been restrained by holding it in a mailed glove until it stops struggling will swim for only 30 minutes before giving up. Here inducing a state of learned helplessness by restraining the animal has seriously interfered with what we might describe as the animal's will to live.

Turning now to some human examples of the effects of helplessness, in a simple experiment Hiroto and Seligman (cited in Seligman, 1975) demonstrated its effects on problem solving. They did this by first giving one group of students problems that they could not solve and another group of students problems that they could. They then asked the students to place their fingers in a 'finger shuttle box'. By moving their fingers in this box, they could terminate a very loud noise. Hiroto and Seligman found that those students who had had solvable problems rapidly escaped noise. Those who had unsolvable problems passively accepted the noise and made no attempts to initiate any responses that might end it.

To take another example, Seligman reports a study of elderly persons entering residential homes. Here those who, for various reasons, were *forced* to enter residential care were compared with those who were *choosing* to enter residential care. Once admitted to a residential home it was found that the death rate amongst those who were given no choice in the matter was significantly higher than that in those who were exercising choice. (Death rate was recorded within 10 weeks of admission, and the difference in death rate was not caused by differences in physical health between the 'choice' and 'no choice' groups.)

In general terms Seligman's work demonstrates that when people pass through significant and, in some cases relatively minor, experiences that demonstrate to them that they do not control or influence their environment, this will adversely affect:

1. their motivation – as was the case with Seligman's dogs, they may lack initiative and appear depressed;
2. their mental clarity – they will have difficulty solving problems and, like the dogs that were dragged over the wall of the shuttle box, will find it difficult to discern the conditions necessary for success;
3. their physical health – they are much more likely to fall ill and die.

The conclusion that we can draw from Seligman's work is that receiving an operant reward provides evidence to both animals and people that they control significant aspects of their environment.

With this conclusion in mind we can give another reason for the importance of secondary reinforcers. Secondary rein-

forcers such as affection, money and so on gain their reinforcing properties not only from their association with primary
sources of reward, such as food and drink, but also from the
fact that they lead to important forms of control over the environment. Forms of control that affection, money and so on
create may be more important than the fact that they derive
their value from association with primary reinforcers.

BASIC THEMES IN BEHAVIOURISM AND LINKS WITH THE INTRODUCTION

Basic themes in Part III

In the second chapter in this section a warning was given about the lack of adequate testing of self-help programmes. People who try these programmes out and who find they do not work may blame not the programme but themselves. Such people may easily fall foul of the kind of mental processes that cognitive therapists try to expose. Believing in the validity of a self-help programme, a person may approach it with perfectionist standards and any degree of failure, even if it is relatively small, may be construed as a personal 'disaster'.

Other attitudes condemned by cognitive therapists may also occur in the unsuccessful application of a self-help programme – regarding failure as an indication of the kind of person one is, feeling one 'must', 'ought' or 'should' succeed and so on. Not only are these attitudes unfortunate in their own right but they are also particularly so if it is the programme itself that is at fault.

Much of the material in the chapter on personal change complements the material covered on cognitive therapy and can be used in conjunction with it. For example, the approach taken to the analysis of problematic emotions in the chapter on personal change is similar to that taken in one of the suggested homework assignments in cognitive therapy.

The principles of personal change explained in Chapter 10 have clear parallels in Chapter 11, which deals with the problematic behaviour of children. The analysis of personal behaviour is to some extent repeated and embellished in the analysis of a child's behaviour, particularly when examining relations between behaviour, antecedents and consequences.

Clearly much of the experimental work done by behaviourists applies to children. Of particular importance are the experiments which show that partial reinforcement leads to persistent behaviour and, against the predictions of common sense, punishment does not necessarily eliminate unwanted behaviour.

Finally Seligman's work on the importance of control links with many of the issues discussed in previous chapters. For example, the successful outcome of cognitive therapy is the production of controllable emotions and the endpoint of a behaviourist self-change programme is the individual's management of the conditions that control him or her.

Behaviourism and the change process

There are two ways in which the principles of behaviourism can be applied. The first is to create a highly structured environment in which seriously problematic behaviour can be brought under control. Although this use of behaviourism is not necessarily confined to children, a problem child illustrates well what it has to offer. A child who is totally out of control, beyond the influence of parents, teachers and peers, is frightening not just to other people but also to him or herself. Such a child will benefit from removal from the context in which the problem thrives to one (such as a residential home) in which clearly specified behaviour is followed by clearly identifiable rewards. Initially this behaviour should be rewarded frequently; with time, in order to make it persist, it should be rewarded less and less frequently on a partial reinforcement schedule.

This change in the child illustrates, in a more literal sense than that discussed in the introduction, the influence of change of context as a means of destabilising a problem and making it more amenable to change.

The second use to which behaviourism can be put is a more common-sense one. There is clearly a convincing logic in the principles of cognitive therapy, self-change and behaviourist approaches to children's behaviour. These principles can be used by a person without his or her necessarily being a convinced behaviourist.

The historical and social context of behaviourism

Of the three perspectives covered in this book, the behaviourist is the one which has historically sought to be most firmly rooted in scientific method. As a system that explains psychological processes, it has aimed to deal only with observable facts.

Although this aim is a straightforward one, its simplicity is more apparent than real. Behaviourism has traditionally rested on the link between an environmental circumstance – the stimulus – and the behaviour it produces – the response. Defining the nature of stimulus and response, particularly in the case of human beings, has proved exceedingly difficult. What, for example, is the stimulus of this page? Is it simply a set of marks made by printer's ink on a white background? Once we go beyond such matters and become concerned with what you make of this page, the idea of a stimulus is no longer simple and easy to define, observe or quantify. Not only does describing the exact nature of a stimulus present problems but so also does defining or observing a response – as is shown by any attempt to assess your response to this page.

Behind the behaviourist's traditional preoccupation with scientific method has been the desire to produce a foolproof method of creating knowledge. Many have believed that by following experimental methods that rely on simple observation, useful knowledge will inevitably be created (Toulmin, 1972). Those who have studied the matter (Polyani, 1962; Kuhn, 1970) have concluded that this is not how scientific insights have been achieved. Intuition, innovation, creativity and even unpopularity have a role to play.

As we have seen pure behaviourism is being diluted by more mentalistic concepts. This is a trend that is no doubt likely to continue because Skinner, the foremost and most brilliant propounder of the behaviourist philosophy (Skinner, 1974), is no longer with us to be its standard bearer.

FURTHER READING

On cognitive therapy

1. Dryden, W. (1984) *Rational–Emotive Therapy: Fundamentals and Innovations*. Beckenham, Kent: Croom Helm.

This is useful introduction to both rational–emotive therapy and cognitive therapy.

On self-change

1. Watson, D.L. and Tharp, R.G. (1992) *Self-directed Behavior: Self-modification for Personal Adjustment*. Pacific Park, Calif: Brooks/Cole.

This a readable, comprehensive and thorough treatment of this subject.

On behavioural treatment of children

1. Herbert, M. (1981) *Behavioural Treatment of Problem Children: A Practice Manual*. London: Academic Press.

This is a very systematic account of how to deal with problematic behaviour in children. It is probably too systematic to be read from cover to cover but can be used as a reference text.

On behaviourism

1. Skinner, B.F. (1974) *About Behaviorism*. London: Jonathan Cape.

If you wish to learn to think as a behaviourist, this is the book to read. By what could be a philosophical sleight of hand, Skinner again and again reduces experience to a few basic behaviourist ideas. He does this in a way that is a wonder to behold.

SOME COMPARISONS BETWEEN HUMANISTIC PSYCHOLOGY, PSYCHOANALYSIS AND BEHAVIOURISM

SUMMARY

Three examples of the way in which one perspective can be related to another are given. First, there is an example of the kind of criticism one perspective is inclined to make of another; then there is an illustration of how one perspective would explain or 'explain away' another; and finally there is an example of how one perspective can make a contribution to another.

Before comparing perspectives with each other, there is a short section outlining research on the effectiveness of psychological interventions.

Research on the effectiveness of methods of change

Many investigations have been carried out into the effectiveness of the kinds of method of change described in this book (Bergin and Garfield, 1994) but conducting research into any measure of success is difficult. One must take into account such matters as the type and intensity of the problem, how motivated the client is to change, whether the problem would have disappeared of its own accord given time, how long the method of change is to be applied, what constitutes improvement, how long beneficial changes persist, whether relapses occur and so on.

Studies of effectiveness have tried to take into account these complexities but further research is needed. In spite of this it can be stated with some certainty that psychological methods of change are effective. Indeed in some instances they are more effective than change brought about by medication (some forms of cognitive therapy being superior in the treatment of depression) and education (Lambert and Bergin, 1994).

A useful distinction emerging in this area of research is that between factors common to any psychological intervention and those which are associated with a specific technique, method or theoretical perspective. Since many of the intervention described in this book are used by trained practitioners and all practitioners must make a relationship with their clients, one of the common factors is the quality of the practitioner–client relationship. The effect of this has long been known. For example, if two behaviourists are using the same technique with a group of clients to resolve the same problem, the behaviourist who makes a good relationship with his or her clients (such as the one seen in person-centred therapy) will have a significantly better success rate than the one who makes a poor relationship (Beech, 1969).

Where distinctive methods have been compared, behaviourist techniques have generally been found to be more successful than others. However, where possible biases in the research process have been eliminated, the advantages of behaviourist techniques over others have been found to be marginal. At this stage it is reasonable to assume that all methods are successful, although some may offer more for particular problems with particular clients. That all methods are successful is a conclusion that one could draw from the explanation of change given at the beginning of this book.

Carkhuff and Berenson (1977) offer a conceptual approach that links the common factor of relationship with the effect of more specific techniques and methods. They suggest that clients who have a psychological problem require two things. First, they must understand the position they are in. Customarily a person does not have this kind of understanding. People who tell their story often have only a superficial grasp of their problem. So that a person can understand the position he or she is in, a method is required that will bring about a reasonably prolonged exploration of the problem, with the aim of discovering aspects of it that were previously unrecognised. Such a method is offered in person-centred therapy.

Once a person comes to an adequate understanding, this more developed grasp of the psychological problem may be sufficient to produce the change that is desired or necessary. When it does not produce change or does not do so sufficiently quickly, Carkhuff and Berenson suggest a second step is needed. A person needs to know how to progress from the point of deeper understanding to his or her desired goal. In many cases in order to change a person must know the steps necessary for change. Both the psychoanalytic and the behaviourist perspectives offer such steps.

A comparison of the humanistic and psychoanalytic approaches

Psychoanalysis has rightly been criticised for being difficult to test or experimentally investigate (Eysenck, 1986). We can illustrate this problem in the following way. Freud suggested a link between an infant being praised for bowel movements and the appearance in childhood and adulthood of the trait of generosity. Suppose we conduct a study that examines this relationship, following up infants who were praised and those who were not over (say) a 20-year period. If, as is likely, we fail to find a sufficiently strong relationship to support Freud's hypothesis (Kline, 1972), a psychoanalyst can invoke the principle of reaction formation (see Chapter 8) to explain away what we have found; that is, he or she can state that generosity exists at one level of the personality but not at another, more conscious, overt level, where it is negated. This explanation means that when the theory's predictions are disproved, a psychoanalyst can explain this result in a manner that leaves the theory intact.

This problem with psychoanalysis does not rule out the possibility that human nature is so complex that reaction formation does occur and that, in some circumstances, invoking it as an explanation is legitimate. For this reason some psychoanalysts openly admit that the principles by which they operate are not essentially scientific (Casement, 1990).

In contrast to the psychoanalytic approach, that of humanistic psychologists is much more empirically based. The conditions of person-centred therapy, for example, have been thoroughly investigated and have been found to be associated with the kinds of improvement in the client that Rogers identified (Mearns, 1993).

A second important difference between psychoanalysis and humanistic psychology concerns the role of conscious and unconscious processes. Conscious examination of present thoughts and feelings in humanistic psychology is the basis of a deeper understanding, which will bring about change. In contrast psychoanalysis is concerned with those dynamic forces in a person's unconscious which govern or rule the present, and these can only be examined indirectly through free association and dream analysis.

Like any well-developed system of thought, psychoanalysis can offer an explanation of why humanistic psychology will or will not produce results, and humanistic psychology can similarly return the complement, explaining why psychoanalysis does or does not work. Again if we take examples from therapy, a Rogerian would argue that it is not necessarily the interpretations of the analyst that are important but the empathic responsiveness to the client's problems. The psychoanalyst would maintain that this empathy is in itself insufficient to deal with the client's problems. It is only the basis of that form of care and attention (or containment) that enables the client safely to relive and resolve the problems of the past.

Rather than seeing these psychoanalytic and humanistic explanations as rival ones, we could regard them as contributing to each other. Maslow (1970) complained that psychoanalysis was based on observations not of healthy but of unhealthy individuals. In making this complaint, however, he acknowledged that it did make a contribution to our understanding of 'sick' and 'normal' people. Maslow, incidentally, makes a similar criticism of behaviourism, which deals with motives associated with needs low in his hierarchy but not with those associated with needs in the upper reaches.

In the area of therapy there are a number of concepts that come from both person-centred therapy and psychoanalysis that can throw light on each other. For example, congruence in person-centred therapy relates to the free flow of information within the therapist so that experience is accurately represented in awareness. Resistance, as defined in psychoanalysis (see Chapters 5 and 6), could be regarded as a failure of congruence in the client.

A comparison of psychoanalytic and behaviourist approaches

In the previously made comparison between psychoanalytic and humanistic psychologies, the point was made that it is difficult to test the claims of psychoanalytic theory. As one might suspect this is a criticism made even more strongly by behaviourists. They reject psychoanalysis on the grounds of its untestability and its reference to unobservable realms of psychological activity such as the unconscious.

When taken to its logical extreme a psychoanalyst's search for the meaning underlying behaviour results in the belief that no behaviour is to be taken at face value; everything is open to interpretation. Superficially behaviourism could be regarded as adopting the opposite stance: it is not what lies behind behaviour but behaviour itself that is of the utmost importance. Hence a major focus of concern should be the simple acts or responses that are made to certain environmental circumstances or stimuli.

As we have seen (in 'Some basic themes in behaviourism') this behaviourist analysis initially seems to be simple and straightforward until we attempt to define words such as 'stimulus' and 'response'. In practice stating just what these terms represent is extremely difficult. Although a behaviourist could criticise a psychoanalyst for being obsessed with the meaning that lies behind everything, the psychoanalyst could in turn suggest that, in falling back on the apparently simple concepts of stimulus and response, the behaviourist has tried to escape from the problem of what things mean but has in fact failed to do so.

In psychoanalysis a person is directed inward and backward in time and the reality of personality traits that are seen as rooted in the past are taken for granted. In behaviourism a person is directed outward to current situations that are regarded as potent cues for and causes of behaviour; personality traits are by no means assumed to be the most valid terms for describing what is significant about a person and his or her problems.

We can, of course, investigate psychoanalysis using behaviourism, looking at it in terms of the context or situation in which it is practised. Perhaps the regressive preoccupations of the client undergoing psychoanalysis should not surprise us when we see how the client, with childlike submission, is requested by the therapist to lie on a couch and follow the therapist's instructions to freely associate.

The psychoanalyst can counter this criticism with a similar one. The authoritative use of behaviourist principles to bring about change, in the administration of rewards for example, reproduces exactly those conditions that will trigger transference. And it is this more than anything else that needs to be adequately resolved.

Although in their pure forms they must be regarded as extremely far apart, psychoanalysis and behaviourism have some elements in their perspectives that could be used in a complementary manner. For example, one concerns itself primarily with the origins of problems and the other with their maintenance. Although behaviourism does sometimes give attention to a person's reinforcement history, it is very often more preoccupied with what is maintaining a problem.

A fertile ground for mutual theoretical contributions is that of identification and modelling. The former is (as defined earlier in this book) a psychoanalytic term for unconscious imitation. The latter is the behaviourist term for a very similar process, although one having a better researched pedigree.

A comparison of humanistic psychology and behaviourism

Humanistic psychology contrasts with behaviourism in its heavy emphasis on the importance of relationships in fostering emotional wellbeing and psychological growth. In person-centred therapy, for example, the relationship is one which seeks to invest power in the client. In contrast, particularly when it is used on those occupying subordinate positions, such as children or the mentally disordered, behaviourism can be described as manipulative. Behaviourists counter this criticism by suggesting that they are merely doing efficiently what others who do not fully appreciate the principles of behaviourism do inefficiently. They can also point out that although person-centred therapists can boast about empowering their clients, they give their clients no choice over the *type* of relationship they offer. If you are offered person-centred therapy but wish for advice about your problem (the kind that might come from a cognitive therapist), you will be denied this.

Some therapists using the person-centred approach claim that the client's sensitivity to the detail or subtle nuances of their feelings can be such that they are able to discover ways in which they are incorrectly constructing their view of reality (Rice, 1984). This includes the discovery of exactly those failures that cognitive therapists have described – the demands placed on self, for example, by the use of words like 'must', 'ought' and 'should'. This process of working from emotions to thoughts is the reverse of the one that cognitive therapists suggest is so important, namely working from faulty thinking to its emotional consequences.

Behaviourists can explain Rogerian therapy as a form of conditioning. Certain problems associated with anxiety are discussed with a therapist who is warm, open and accepting. Gradually the positive presence of the therapist becomes associated with the problems that are discussed. This eliminates the client's anxieties and, with these out of the way, the client can talk more freely and obviously feels more comfortable.

Many of the criticisms that humanistic psychology and behaviourism might make of each other can be developed into theoretical contributions that one could make to the other. Two examples have already been mentioned. One is the importance of a good relationship when applying behaviourist techniques. The other, which mirrors what was said in the comparison made of psychoanalysis and behaviourism, is in the area of modelling. Several references were actually made in the chapter on person-centred therapy to the kind of model that a Rogerian therapist can provide for a client and how the client can benefit from this.

We know from Seligman's work (1975; Mikulincer, 1994) that the control that people exercise over their environment contributes to their mental clarity, their emotional stability and their physical health. Both the client in therapy being attentively listened to by a therapist and the self-actualised person exercise control over their environments that enhances their psychological health.

REFERENCES

Balint, M. (1952) *Primary Love and Psychoanalytic Technique*. London: Tavistock Publications.

Bandura, A. (1977) Self-efficacy: toward a unifying theory of behavioral change. *Psychological Review*, **84**, 191–215.

Bandura, A. (1989) Self-regulation of motivation through internal standards and goal systems. In Pervin, L. (ed.) *Goal Concepts in Personality and Social Psychology*. Hillsdale, N.J.: Erlbaum Associates.

Bateson, G. (1972) *Steps to an Ecology of Mind*. New York: Ballantine Books.

Beck, A.T., Rush, A.J., Shaw, B.F. and Emery, G. (1979) *Cognitive Therapy of Depression*. New York: Guilford Press.

Beech, H.R. (1969) *Changing Man's Behaviour*. Harmondsworth: Penguin Books.

Bellack, A.S., Rozensky, R. and Schwartz, J. (1974) A comparison of two forms of self-monitoring in a behavioral weight reduction programme. *Behavior Therapy*, **5**, 523–30.

Berger, P.L. (1966) *Invitation to Sociology*. Harmondsworth: Penguin Books.

Bergin, A.E. and Garfield, S.L., (eds) (1994) *Handbook of Psychotherapy and Behavior Change*. Chichester: John Wiley.

Bion, W.R. (1967) *Second Thoughts*. New York: Aronson.

Bugental, J.F.T. (1976) *The Search for Existential Identity*. San Francisco: Jossey-Bass.

Cameron, N.A. and Magaret, A. (1951) *Behavior Pathology*. Boston: Houghton Mifflin.

Caplan, G. (1964) *Principles of Preventive Psychiatry*. London: Tavistock Publications.

Caputi, N. (1984) *Guide to the Unconscious*. Birmingham, Ala.: Religous Education Press.

Carkhuff, R.R. and Berenson, B.G. (1977) *Beyond Counselling and Therapy*. New York: Holt, Rinehart and Winston.

Carp, F.M. (1969) Senility or garden-variety maladjustment? *Journal of Gerontology*, **24**, 221–8.

Cartledge, G. and Milburn, J.F. (1980) *Teaching Social Skills to Children*. Oxford: Pergamon.

Casement, P. (1985) *On Learning from the Patient*. London: Tavistock Publications.

Casement, P. (1990) *Further Learning from the Patient*. London: Tavistock Publications.

Cashdan, S. (1988) *Object Relations Therapy*. London: Norton.

Conte, H.R. and Plutchik, R. (1995) *Ego Defenses: Theory and Measurement*. London: John Wiley.

Csikszentmihayli, M. (1975) *Beyond Boredom and Anxiety*. San Francisco: Jossey-Bass.

Csikszentmihayli, M. (1992) *Flow: The Psychology of Happiness*. London: Rider.

Csikszentmihayli, M. and Csikszentmihayli, I.S. (eds) (1988) *Optimal Experience*. Cambridge: Cambridge University Press.

Dicks, H.V. (1967) *Marital Tensions*. London: Routledge & Kegan Paul.

Dryden, W. (1984) *Rational–Emotive Therapy: Fundamentals and Innovations*. Beckenham, Kent: Croom Helm.

Dryden, W. and Golden, W. (eds) (1986) *Cognitive–Behavioural Approaches to Psychotherapy*. London: Harper and Row.

Eichenbaum, L. and Orbach, S. (1984) *What Do Women Want?* London: Fontana.

Ellenberger, H. (1957) The unconscious before Freud. *Bulletin of the Menninger Clinic*, **21**(3), 12–21.

Ellis, A. (1979) The theory of rational–emotive therapy. In Ellis, A. and Whiteley, J.M. (eds) *Theoretical and Empirical Foundations of Rational–Emotive Therapy*. Monterey, Calif.: Brooks/Cole.

Ellis, A. (1993) The use of rational humorous songs in psychotherapy. In Fry, W.F. and Salameh, W.A. (eds) *Handbook of Humor and Psychotherapy*. Sarasota, Fla: Professional Resource Exchange.

Ellis, A. and Bernard, M.A.(eds) (1983) *Rational–Emotive Approaches to the Problems of Childhood*. London: Plenum Press.

Eysenck, H.J. (1967) *The Biological Basis of Personality*. Springfield, Ill.: Charles Thomas.

Eysenck, H.J. (1970) *Crime and Personality*. London: Paladin.

Eysenck, H.J. (1984) Crime and personality. In Muller, D.J., Blackman, D.E. and Chapman, A.J. (eds) *Psychology and Law*. Chichester: John Wiley.

Eysenck, H.J. (1986) *Decline and Fall of the Freudian Empire*. Harmondsworth: Penguin Books.

Eysenck, H.J. (1987) Personality theory and the problems of criminality. In McGurk, B.J., Thornton, D.M. and Williams, M. (eds) *Applying Psychology to Imprisonment: Theory and Practice*. London: HMSO.

Fine, R. (1973) Psychoanalysis. In Corsini, R. *Current Psychotherapies*. Tasca, Ill.: Peacock.

Foulds, G.A. (1965) *Personality and Personal Illness*. London: Tavistock Publications.

Freud, A. (1936) *The Ego and the Mechanisms of Defense*. London: Hogarth Press and the Institute of Psychoanalysis.

Freud, S. (1910) *The Future Prospects of Psychotherapy*. London: Hogarth Press.

Freud S. (1949) *An Outline of Psychoanalysis*. New York: Norton.

Fromm, E. (1962) *The Art of Loving*. London: Unwin Books.

Fromm, E. (1982) *Greatness and Limitations of Freud's Thought*. London: Cape.

Gendlin, E.T. (1967) Therapeutic procedures in dealing with schizophrenics. In Rogers, C.R. *et al.* (eds) *The Therapeutic Relationship and its Impact: a Study of Psychotherapy with Schizophrenics*. Maddison: University of Wisconsin Press.

Gottschalk, L. A. (1989) *How to Do Self-Analysis and Other Self-Psychotherapies*. London: Jason Aronson.

Hafner, J.R. (1985) *Marriage and Mental Illness: A Sex-Role Perspective*. New York: Guilford Press.

Hartrup, W.W. (1974) Aggression in children: developmental perspectives. *American Psychologist*, **29**, 336-41.

Herbert, M. (1981) *Behavioural Treatment of Problem Children: A Practice Manual*. London: Academic Press.

Horney, K. (1942) *Self-analysis*. New York: Norton.

Howitt, D. and Owusu-Bempah, J. (1994) *The Racism of Psychology*. London: Harvester Wheatsheaf.

Jahoda, M. (1958) *Current Conceptions of Positive Mental Health*. New York: Basic Books.

Jehu, D. (1966) *Learning Theory and Social Work*. New York: Humanities Press.

Keeney, B.P. (1983) *The Aesthetics of Change*. New York: Guilford Press.

Klein, M. (1952) Some theoretical conclusions regarding the emotional life of the infant. In Klein, M. (ed.) (1975) *Envy and Gratitude and Other Works, 1946–1963*. New York: Delacorter Press.

Klein, M. and Tribich, D. (1981) Kernberg's object-relations theory: a critical evaluation. *International Journal of Psychoanalysis*, **62**, 27–43.

Kline, P. (1972) *Fact and Fantasy in Freudian Theory*. London: Methuen.

Kuhn, T.S. (1970) *The Structure of Scientific Revolutions*. Chicago: Chicago University Press.

Laing. R.D. (1969) *Self and Others*. Harmondsworth: Penguin Books.

Lambert, M.J. and Bergin, A.E. (1994) The effectiveness of psychotherapy. In Bergin, A.E. and Garfield, S.L. (eds) *Handbook of Psychotherapy and Behavior Change*. Chichester: John Wiley.

Leitaer, G. (1993) Authenticity, congruence and transparency. In Brazier, D. (ed.) *Beyond Carl Rogers*. London: Constable.

Lewinsohn, P.M. and Libet, J. (1972) Pleasant events, activity schedules and depression. *Journal of Abnormal Psychology*, **79**, 291–5.

Marris, P. (1986) *Loss and Change*. London: Routledge & Kegan Paul.

Maslow, A.H. (1968) *Towards a Psychology of Being*. New York: Van Nostrand.

Maslow, A.H. (1970) *Motivation and Personality*. London: Harper and Row.

Maslow, A.H. (1973) *The Farther Reaches of Human Nature*. Harmondsworth: Penguin Books.

Massie, H. N. (1982) Affective development and the organisation of the mother–infant behaviour from the perspective of psychopathology. In, Tronick, E. Z. (ed) *Social Interchange in Infancy: Affect, Cognition and Communication*. Baltimore: University Park Press.

Matson, J.L. and Ollendick, T.H. (1977) Issues in toilet training normal children. *Behavior Therapy*, **8**, 549–53.

May, R. (1972) *Love and Will*. London: Fontana.

Mearns, D. (1993) The core conditions. In Dryden, W. (ed.) *Questions and Answers in Counselling in Action*. London: Sage.

Menaker, E. (1991) Questioning the sacred cow of transference. In Curtis, R.C. and Stricker, G. (eds) *How People Change Inside and Outside Therapy*. London: Plenum Press.

Mikulincer, M. (1994) *Human Learned Helplessness: A Coping Perspective*. London: Plenum Press.

Parry, G. (1990) *Coping with Crises*. Leicester: British Psychological Society.

Piaget, J. (1954) *The Construction of Reality in the Child*. New York: Basic Books.

Polanyi, M. (1962) *Personal Knowledge: Towards a Post Critical Philosophy*. Chicago: Chicago University Press.

Rabin, C. (1981) A behavioural perspective on the scapegoat theory. *International Journal of Behavioural Social Work and Abstracts*. **1**(2), 109–24.

Rathunde, K. (1988) Optimal experience and the family context. In Csikszentmihayli, M. and Csikszentmihayli, I. (eds) *Optimal Experience*. Cambridge: Cambridge University Press.

Reich, A. (1951) On Counter-Transference. *International Journal of Psychoanalysis*. **32**, 25–31.

Rice, L.N. (1984) Client-tasks in client-centred therapy. In Levant, R.F. and Schien, J.M. (eds) *Client-centred Therapy and the Person-centred Approach: New Directions in Theory, Research and Practice*. New York: Preager.

Robinson, L. (1995) *Psychology and Social Workers: Black Perspectives*. London: Routledge.

Rogers, C.R. (1951) *Client-centred Therapy*. Boston: Houghton Mifflin.

Rogers, C.R. (1959) A theory of therapy, personality and interpersonal relationships. In Koch, S. (ed.) *Psychology: The Study of a Science*, vol. 3. New York: McGraw Hill.

Rogers, C.R. (1961) *On Becoming a Person: A Therapist's View of Psychotherapy*. Boston: Houghton Mifflin.

Rogers, C.R. (1966) Client-centred therapy. In Arieti, S. (ed.) *American Handbook of Psychiatry*, vol. 3. New York: Basic Books.

Rogers, C.R. (1970) *On Encounter Groups*. London: Harper and Row.

Rogers, C.R. (1978) *Carl Rogers on Personal Power*. London: Constable.

Rogers, C.R. (1980) *A Way of Being*. Boston: Houghton Mifflin.

Rogers, C.R. (1983) *Freedom to Learn for the Eighties*. Columbus, Ohio: Merrill.

Rogers, C.R. and Stevens, B. (1973) *Person to Person*. London: Souvenir Press.

Rosen G. M. (1982) Self-help approaches to management. In Blankstein, K.R. and Polivy, J. (eds) *Self-Control and Self-Modification of Emotional Behavior*. London: Plenum Press.

Rubin, L. (1985) *Intimate Strangers*. London: Fontana.

Schultz, D. (1977) *Growth Psychology: Models of the Healthy Personality*. London: Van Nostrand.

Seligman, M.E.P. (1975) *Helplessness*. San Francisco: Freeman and Co.

Shepherd, M., Oppenheim, B. and Mitchell, S. (1971) *Childhood Behaviour and Mental Health*. London: London University Press.

Skinner, B.F. (1974) *About Behaviorism*. London: Jonathan Cape.

Southgate, J. (1987) Sigmund Freud – the pioneer of self-analysis. *Journal of the Institute of Self-Analysis*, **1**(1), 38–73.

Storr, A. (1963) *The Integrity of Personality*. Harmondsworth: Penguin Books.

Thorne, B. (1991) *Person-centred Counselling: Therapeutic and Spiritual Dimensions*. London: Whurr.

Toulmin, S. (1972) *Human Understanding*. London: Routledge & Kegan Paul.

Trilling, L. and Markus, S. (eds) (1964) *The Life and Work of Sigmund Freud*. Harmondsworth: Penguin Books.

Van Leeuwen, M.S. (1985) *The Person in Psychology*. Leicester: Inter-Varsity Press.

Wachtel, P.L. (1991) The role of 'accomplices' in preventing and facilitating change. In Curtis, R.C. and Stricker, G. (eds) *How People Change Inside and Outside Therapy*. London: Plenum Press.

Watson, J.B. (1913) Psychology as a behaviourist views it. *Psychological Review*, **20**, 158–77.

Watson, D.L. and Tharp, R.G. (1977) *Self-directed Behaviour: Self-modification for Personal Adjustment*. Monterey, Calif.: Brooks/Cole.

Watzlawick, P., Weakland, J.H. and Fisch, R. (1974) *Change: Principles of Problem Formation and Resolution*. London: Norton.

Wilkinson, S. (1986) *Feminist Social Psychology*. Milton Keynes: Open University Press.

Winnicott, D.W. (1958) *Collected Papers: Through Paediatrics to Psycho-Analysis*. London: Tavistock Publications.

Winnicott, D.W. (1971) *Playing and Reality*. London: Tavistock Publications.

Yallom, I.D. (1980) *Existential Therapy*. New York: Basic Books.

INDEXES

There are three indexes below, one listing authors, a second listing ideas and concepts and a third listing examples. I have included the third index, covering all important examples, because often a reader associates an idea or a principle with the example that explains it. Such a reader, when wishing to locate an idea, may find it helpful to do so by referring to the examples index.

AUTHOR INDEX

253

SUBJECT INDEX

Index of Examples

257